Arthur B. Shostak is an Associate Professor of Social Sciences at Drexel University, Philadelphia and is a close student of issues in social change and social planning. His edited works include: *Blue-Collar World* (1964), *New Perspectives on Poverty* (1965), *Sociology in Action* (1966), and *Sociology and Student Life* (1970). The author of *Blue-Collar Life* (1969), he has two additional books at press: *Putting Sociology to Work* and *Modern Social Reforms*. A sometime consultant to OEO, Job Corps, social audit designers, computer simulation game-builders, and a wide variety of other parties, he is presently researching material for a monograph on New Towns here and abroad.

Jon Van Til is the Executive Director of the Pennsylvania Law and Justice Institute, and was for six years a member of the Sociology faculty at Swarthmore College. As an applied sociologist, he has been active in welfare and housing politics in Philadelphia, and currently heads an agency that seeks to create a partnership of officials, citizens, and educators for reform in criminal justice in the Philadelphia metropolitan area. His study of urban governing structures in Philadelphia will be published by The Brookings Institution in 1974.

Sally Bould Van Til is an Assistant Professor of Sociology at the University of Delaware. A specialist in poverty, social policy, and social stratification, she has studied programs of income maintenance and welfare in the United States, England, and France. She is currently studying the economic activity of the poor and nonpoor by an analysis of a large-scale national survey. She has published articles on citizen participation and problems of poverty.

PRIVILEGE IN AMERICA
An End to Inequality?

ARTHUR B. SHOSTAK
JON VAN TIL
SALLY BOULD VAN TIL

> We are moving from an age in which we could afford just to state our ideals about human rights to an age when these ideals must become realities if the society is going to function at all.
>
> Robert Theobald,
> *The Challenge to Affluence*

PRENTICE-HALL, INC.   Englewood Cliffs, New Jersey

Library of Congress Cataloging in Publication Data

SHOSTAK, ARTHUR B
   Privilege in America.

  (A Spectrum Book)
  Bibliography: p.
  1. Economic assistance, Domestic—United States.
  2. Social classes—United States. 3. Equality.
I. Van Til, Jon. II. Van Til, Sally Bould.
III. Title.
HC110.P63S52   301.44′0973   79-16111
ISBN 0-13-711119-3
ISBN 0-13-711101-0 (pbk)

© 1973 by Prentice-Hall, Inc., Englewood Cliffs, New Jersey. A SPECTRUM BOOK. All rights reserved. No part of this book may be reproduced in any form or by any means without permission in writing from the publisher. Printed in the United States of America.

10 9 8 7 6 5 4 3 2 1

PRENTICE-HALL INTERNATIONAL, INC. (*London*)
PRENTICE-HALL OF AUSTRALIA PTY. LTD. (*Sydney*)
PRENTICE-HALL OF CANADA LTD. (*Toronto*)
PRENTICE-HALL OF INDIA PRIVATE LIMITED (*New Delhi*)
PRENTICE-HALL OF JAPAN, INC. (*Tokyo*)

PREFACE

This book is about an ancient dream of human beings—the reduction of social inequality, a dream very much alive in our own place and our own time. Indeed, perceptions of social inequality in America are undergoing extraordinary revisions. People once cowed are now aggressive (Wounded Knee, and the USS *Kitty Hawk*); people once timid are newly assertive (the well-off liberation-seeking women of the National Organization for Women, and the poorly-off livelihood-seeking women of the National Welfare Rights Organization). The call for the reduction of inequality is also heard in other comparably novel corners in the land. "Hard-hats," for example, demand a form of equality that they imagine the better-off enjoy (freedom from fear of urban crime); many of the better-off, in turn, demand a form of equality that they associate with manual workers (freedom to "go ethnic," and thereby to gain some distinctiveness in a bland, homogenized mass society). Certain environmentalists call for a new equality in antimaterialism, for a mass conversion to the dictum that "less is more." Certain anarchists, on the contrary, call ironically for the celebration of a cybernetic cornucopia, for they contend that only postscarcity affluence makes equality in well-being both attainable and retainable.

Our book is divided into three sections. In the first part, we review the origins of inequality and conclude that it is *not* an inevitable aspect of social life, but rather a phenomenon that can be altered and affected by purposive human action. In the second part we examine the major ways in which equality and inequality are explained and justified, particularly the ideologies of liberalism, conservatism, populism, and socialism. In the concluding section we examine specific programs aimed at the reduction of inequality and ponder the chances of their adoption.

We, the authors, are convinced that prevailing inequality forms a basic flaw in American society, and that it can and must be reduced. We are neither starry-eyed liberal optimists nor utopian radicals. Each of us has worked with groups of poor and working-class persons who have sought to advance their interests against prevailing conceptions of inequality and believes that this struggle must be continued and augmented. We invite our readers to join in this struggle, addressing and influencing what we consider to be *the* social issue of our times.

The book is truly a joint project. Jon Van Til took primary responsibility for the first section, Arthur B. Shostak for the second, and Sally Bould Van Til for the third. Each of us exchanged comments and assisted the others in the preparation of the book. We are hopeful that our collaboration has produced a book that both informs and inspires social action. There is a great need for intelligent and far-sighted politics in our time. We offer this book as one small step toward its construction.

ACKNOWLEDGMENTS

This volume originated with a suggestion from Prentice-Hall editor Michael Hunter that Art Shostak, a coeditor of a 1965 Spectrum Books anthology, *New Perspectives on Poverty*, update and revise that earlier work. Stimulated by a characteristically provocative *New York Times* Op-ed Page essay of Tom Wicker's, Michael nurtured the project and gave it early direction, regular prodding, and unfailing encouragement—for all of which he has our considerable gratitude.

We have been aided in preparing this volume under a firm deadline by the assistance of several talented persons. David E. Nicholls of the United States Department of Agriculture, an economist, prepared the first draft of Chapter 2, of which he is coauthor. His enthusiasm, scholarship, and conformance to our time line have earned our appreciation. Cyndi Turner, talented far beyond her years, provided excellent editorial assistance for Parts I and III. Professor Howard Harlan of the University of Delaware provided an insightful reading of Chapters 7 and 8, and Mary Winter assisted in the background research in the preparation of those chapters. Much of the draft was typed by Irmgard Flaschka. Arthur Shostak received special academic and administrative aid from Susan L. Marker, whose enthusiasm helped at many critical moments. The efforts of all are gratefully acknowledged, for they were timely and helpful.

Finally, a number of graduate students in a course that Arthur Shostak taught in Social Stratification as a Visiting Professor at the Graduate School of the New School for Social Research (Spring 1971) contributed much—though we did not realize then that this book would eventuate three years later. Excellent papers by Richard Lorr, Andrea and Carmen Sirianni, Beverly Lipson, Laurel Butler, Joseph Drew, R. C. Tash, Dolores Blanding, and Patricia Bonfield, among others, lent much solid thought to Shostak's occasional tendencies toward flights of fancy in this field.

CONTENTS

I. INEQUALITY IN AMERICA: THE PROBLEM

1. Social Inequality: How Did We Get Here, Anyway?   1
2. The Magnitude of Inequality   9

II. NEW PERSPECTIVES ON INEQUALITY IN AMERICA

3. Traditional Views: Liberalism and Conservatism   33
4. The Old Populism and America's Old Inequalities   39
5. America's Democratic Socialist Movement   51
6. Ethnicity, Ethnic Power, and Social Inequality   74

III. STRATEGIES FOR THE REDUCTION OF INEQUALITY

7. Strategies to Reduce Poverty and Inequality: An Overview   88
8. Cash-Transfer Programs and the Reduction of Inequality   104
9. An End to Inequality?   128

Annotated Bibliography   144

Index   148

To Arthur's mother, Bessie L. Shostak, who has taught him much about the complexities of social class realities in a democratic Republic.

And to Sally's father, and Jon's father-in-law, Howard Bould, who has shown them that people have a remarkable capacity to grow and change.

I. INEQUALITY IN AMERICA: THE PROBLEM

1
Social Inequality: How Did We Get Here, Anyway?

Jon Van Til

It is customary for social scientists in this country to begin books about equality and inequality with a discussion of why inequality is an inevitable and even necessary aspect of social life. Inequality seems so much a part of our own class-conscious society that it can seem utopian to regard it as anything but inevitable. However, since there are situations in which human beings live in virtual equality, we choose to begin this eclectic volume with an atypical discussion of the social reality of equality. Why is it that a very natural way of organizing society has given way in our own time to a much more inegalitarian social form—with all the attendant costs that tax us so?

Among the most egalitarian societies existent in the world today are those of hunter–gatherer peoples. Societies like the Bushmen of South Africa's Kalahari Desert, the Pygmies of the African Congo, and the Indians of Tierra del Fuego at the tip of South America minimize differences in wealth and possessions among individuals. Thus, when the mutually cooperating Bushmen hunters make a substantial kill, the meat is shared in waves of distribution throughout the entire band. Equality is not absolute in quantitative terms: each person gives "with reasonable generosity in proportion to what he has received" and keeps no more than an "equitable amount for himself." Each person who receives a gift of meat "must give a reciprocal gift of meat at some time in the future."[1]

The Mbuti Pygmies are somewhat more argumentative about the distribution of the catch, but they nonetheless end up sharing rather equally as well: "Survival can be achieved only by the closest cooperation and by an elaborate system of reciprocal obligations which ensures that everyone has some share in the day's catch. Some days one gets more than some of the others, but nobody ever goes without. There is, as often as not, a great deal of squabbling over the division of the game, but that is expected, and nobody tries to take what is not his due." [2]

Individuals in egalitarian societies like those of the Pygmies and the Bushmen are neither especially ranked nor significantly stratified. That is to say, there are just as many positions available in the society that are perceived to be valuable and honorable as there are persons capable of filling them. These positions are not meaningfully ranked in order of their importance or desirability. The absence of stratification here means that adult members of society do not "enjoy differential rights of access to basic resources." [3]

Egalitarian societies tend to develop in areas in which the natural food supply is limited, the population is sparse, and the peoples involved have limited technological sophistication. The basis of widespread sharing in such societies is the felt obligation to return what is given. This obligation, which anthropologists call reciprocity, provides assurance to individuals that their survival will be considered important by their fellows: an individual or family will not be allowed to starve simply because only certain others have been lucky enough to locate food. A web of reciprocal obligation is created in this way within the band, each member of which is aware that he must contribute to the well-being of all his fellow members insofar as the total supply of food permits.

As societies become more complex, both ranking and stratification of consequence begin to appear. Ever more refined distinctions are increasingly made between those with whom sharing is conducted and those beyond the circle of reciprocity. Thus, even in our own society, sharing is still common within the nuclear family, and, in some cases, between members of extended families and even neighbors. However, outside of these small social circles informal sharing rarely exists. Instead, formal institutions such as our tax structure and the local and national welfare systems have been developed to facilitate the limited amount of sharing that takes place in inegalitarian societies.

For many centuries, sophisticated social observers have admiringly wondered at the egalitarianism of the primitive hunter–gatherer societies. Karl Marx, for one, spoke of their condition as "primitive communism," while others have found in their experience the roots of man's golden age, a compelling time before the fall into sin-inviting complexity, religion-toppling technology, and creeping class inequality. Jean-Jacques Rousseau presented a fascinating discourse on the unhappy origins of social inequality, an essay well worth comparing to contemporary findings of social scientists who have more favorably evaluated the "inevitable" development of ranking and stratification.

WHY DOES INEQUALITY APPEAR?

To Rousseau the natural state of man was a state of equality, but also a state in which man's relations with his fellows were not yet developed. Man was seen as "wandering in the forests, without industry, without speech, without home, without war, without ties, without any need of his fellows, without any desire to hurt them, perhaps without recognizing any of them, individually, . . . but sufficing to himself alone." [4] Inequality came into existence when one man fenced off a piece of territory and declared that "this is mine," and also found his claim credited by others. Thus, to Rousseau, the rise of inequality was associated with two important factors—the beginnings of private property and the beginnings of social relations.[5] Interestingly, Rousseau's essay, over two hundred years old, suggests the two major ways in which contemporary social scientists look at inequality and its functions in society. One group of social scientists focuses on inequality as necessary for the development of a complex social system with a high degree of division of labor and functional specialization of roles. A second group of social scientists questions the inevitability of inequality and focuses on the relations between power and inequality, following Rousseau's theme that private property is *the* root of inequality. Differences between these two schools of thought profoundly affect not only the perspectives of social scientists, but also the way in which we ourselves evaluate and analyze social inequality in our private lives and collective experiences.

1. THE CONSENSUS PERSPECTIVE ON INEQUALITY

It is very common in contemporary American society to adopt a "consensus perspective" on inequality. From this point of view, inequality and social stratification are necessary consequences of social differentiation (the increasing division of labor and specialization of roles in society). As the number of positions, or statuses, increases in society, some means is necessary to co-ordinate these units. Two problems for the society thereby arise: recruitment and motivation. People with the skills required to fulfill the roles involved in the division of labor must be channeled into appropriate positions. Consequently, they must be motivated to seek those positions, and discharge faithfully the duties which accompany them.

These problems are resolved in a society, the consensus theorists argue, by providing differential rewards to the occupants of different social positions, rewards that vary with the importance of the status to society, in addition to the degree of scarcity of individuals available to fill the position or the amount of training or talent required for the position. Thus, it is argued, a stratified society is the inevitable consequence of the division of labor that invariably accompanies a society's "coming of age."

Furthermore, most consensus theorists argue, differences in reward that relate to the importance and scarcity of positions play an "integrative" role in society, for these differences in reward contribute to the efficient functioning of society. By serving to enhance the adaptive capacity of society, such stratification makes possible a higher standard of living for all. Not surprisingly, therefore, many consensus theorists find that almost all of society's members normally come to agree that the prevailing system of inequality is acceptable and just, for it appears to be in the interest of all and makes a productive and dynamic social system possible.

Consensus theorists even expect those who do not come out on top in the race for the most important and most highly rewarded social positions to accept their loss and defend the necessity of the system that seems to disadvantage them. Thus, in one study, a worker replied to a question about his views on equality of income:

Now, what would be the advantage of you going twenty years to school, so you wind up making $10,000 a year and me going eight years to school making $10,000? You would be teaching the young men of tomorrow, the leaders of tomorrow, and I would be running a machine. You would then have a lot more responsibility to the country as a whole than I would have. Why shouldn't you be rewarded in proportion? [7]

To summarize the consensus position, then, the form of social stratification and inequality is explained in terms of knitting together a wide range of functionally productive positions in society. A privilege-enhancing pattern of change in social stratification is explained by "unavoidable" changes in the complexity of social organization. Thus, inequality is seen as an inevitable aspect of any complex society, and as a rather productive one.

2. THE CONFLICT PERSPECTIVE ON INEQUALITY

A very different view of stratification and inequality is provided by the modern conflict theorist. Inequality is seen especially as a function of economic power rather than functional differentiation. Naturally, those who control economic power would seek to maintain and perpetuate existent inequality. Indeed, once inequality is allowed to take hold in society, the society rapidly develops a system of political control to maintain differences in rewards structured into the system. Elites, of course, cannot count on a widespread acceptance of a privilege-protecting system of inequality by those not advantaged directly by it; the state is necessary to discipline those who would dare to question the quality of justice of the going social order. Inequality, then, is explained by the interests of those who control production and distribution in society; these interests *must* be defended by state power if they are to be preserved. For if the lower orders are not cowed and controlled effectively, conflict between the few beneficiaries and the multitudes of the lower order will probably result—or so the Establishment fears.

One of the most famous conflict theories of inequality, of course, is that of Karl Marx, who optimistically predicted a series of worldwide revolutions based on resentment about the distribution of power and the amount of inequality in society. Another theorist, and a contemporary of Marx, the colorful anarchist Proud'hon, put the evaluative point quite clearly when he bitterly complained that "property is theft."

Not surprisingly, a heated controversy has long raged between those who adopt the conflict, and those who favor the consensus, perspective on inequality, a controversy at once both intellectual and political in nature. A major way to test the two perspectives is to see how well each analyzes the development of inequality from simple hunter–gatherer societies through to contemporary post-industrial and neocybernetic societies. An adequate theory should be able to explain these four major facts in this societal progression:

1. the classic equality of the primitive hunter–gatherer society;
2. the enormous inequality of preindustrial urban societies, or "peasant" societies, in which a small elite lived in luxury while many from among the masses lived near the brink of starvation;
3. the long-term tendency toward somewhat more widespread manifestations of equality in industrial–urban society, such as that of modern Europe, both East and West, North America, and Japan; and
4. the persistence of reform-oriented conflict over the reduction of inequality in these modern urban–industrial societies.

The consensus perspective is plainly useful in explaining the first two facts. But it gives no particular explanation of why there should be less inequality in industrial–urban than in preindustrial society, nor can it explain the persistence of conflict over the distribution of income and wealth in industrial–urban society. The conflict perspective, on the other hand, is often faulted for not explaining the third fact, the declining inequality in industrial–urban society.

In a fascinating recent volume, the American sociologist Gerhard Lenski has sought to combine the conflict and consensus approaches to the study of the development of social inequality.[8] Representing his work as one of a series of synthesizing volumes between the sociological traditions of conservatism and change, consensus and conflict, Lenski identifies two basic forces, those of need and those of power. Co-operation is clearly needed for production. Hence, "men will share the product of their labors to the extent required to insure the survival and continued productivity of those others whose actions are necessary or beneficial to themselves."[9] Power is crucial in determining what is done with the surplus. Privilege, the share of the surplus received by each individual, is thus crucially determined by power in society. It follows, then, that where societal surplus is small, need will largely determine the pattern of distribution, and where the surplus is large "an increasing proportion of the goods and services available to a society will be distributed on the basis of power."[10]

Now this power does not always take the form of naked oppression, for power in its most effective form *must* be legitimated. This means that society is inclined to transform the rule of might into the rule of right, and power is thereby somewhat more widely shared. Constitutionalism develops, and diverse centers of power emerge along with greater egalitarianism. As long as democratic law is maintained, additional centers of power may develop—though much power remains concentrated. "Powers delegated often become powers lost; once lost they are not easily recovered. Thus it appears that the greater the degree of constitutionalism in society, the less the middle classes function merely as agents of the elite, and the greater their personal independence, autonomy, and security." [11] But elites remain elites, with *real* power—for privilege in society is still a function of power, and not of societal need.

Thus, Lenski explains the "J curve" by which inequality rises from the hunter–gatherer society through the preindustrial urban society and then declines in industrial–urban society. If his theory is applied to the four empirical facts with which we challenged both the conflict and consensus perspectives, we see that the social equality of the hunter-gatherers can be explained by the absence of a food (or wealth) surplus in that type of society. The inequality of feudal peasant society—which Lenski says is the most inegalitarian that man has ever constructed—is explained in turn by the unbridled power of the urban elites to dispose of the societal surplus. Moreover, the increasing equality of urban-industrial society is accounted for by the rise of constitutionalism and the emergence of diverse centers of power. The persistence of conflict over the degree of equality in modern society is explained by the continuing tension between the remaining elites, who have a large share of societal power, and by the increasing political articulation of the middle, working, and even lower classes through constitutional democracy.[12]

By integrating the two major perspectives on the social theory of inequality, Lenski has impressively identified the major forces that can lead to changes in the degree of equality in society. By noting that the presence of multiple centers of power in industrial–urban society restrains the tendency of inequality to increase, Lenski gives us a powerful lever for analysis of contemporary society. Therefore, let us zero in on our own time and place to examine this competition for scarce goods and see what inequality looks like in contemporary American society.

How much inequality is there in the United States today? What sorts of inequalities are most important? How have these patterns been changing? And what are some of the social consequences of these patterns? These are the questions we address in the following chapter, and to which we return again and again elsewhere in the book. For to be alert and concerned in contemporary America is to ask over and again: What of social class today, in a nation that invests millions in pet food, debates the validity of malnutrition data on its poor, tolerates a perilous credibility gap between its haves and have-nots, and, in other critical ways, tempts the fates as we struggle on the "J-curve" of inequality.

1. Warner Marshall, "The Kung Bushmen of the Kalahari Desert" in James L. Gibbs Jr. (ed.) *Peoples of Africa* (New York: Holt, Rinehart and Winston, 1965), p. 254.

2. Colin M. Turnbull, *The Forest People: A Study of the Pygmies of the Congo* (New York: Simon and Schuster, 1962), p. 107.

3. Morton H. Fried, *The Evolution of Political Society: An Essay in Political Anthropology* (New York: Random House, 1967), p. 52.

4. Jean-Jacques Rousseau, "Discourse on the Origin of Inequality" (1754), quoted in Charles W. Hendel, *Jean-Jacques Rousseau: Moralist* (Indianapolis: Bobbs-Merrill, 1934), p. 54.

5. *Ibid.*

6. Kingsley Davis and Wilbert E. Moore, "Some Principles of Stratification," *American Sociological Review*, Volume 10, April, 1945, pp. 242–49.

7. Robert E. Lane, *Political Ideology: Why the American Common Man Believes What He Does* (New York: Free Press of Glencoe, 1962), p. 70.

8. Gerhard Lenski, *Power and Privilege* (New York: McGraw-Hill, 1966).

9. *Ibid.*, p. 44.

10. *Ibid.*, p. 46.

11. *Ibid.*, p. 63.

12. *Ibid.*, chs. 10–11.

2
The Magnitude of Inequality

David E. Nicholls[*]
Jon Van Til

> Presently among the poor and whites on the margin of affluence, gnawing and growing doubts are emerging about the equity of the current distribution of output of our society.[1]

INTRODUCTION

The root of the problem of social and economic inequality in the United States is that the private market distributes private output unequally (though less unequally now than in 1900), and will probably continue to do so in the future. Put another way by 1971 Nobel Prize-winner Simon Kuznets, the problem is the sharp contrast between "top groups attaining too much economic power" and "low income groups who may not be sharing in the country's economic growth." [2]

The magnitude of inequality is commonly measured by separating income earners or possessors of other valuable societal commodities —education, wealth, housing, and property—into categories that represent similar levels of possession of the good in question. A measure of income distribution, the first of our list of important social resources that are distributed unequally, measures the amount

---

[*] David E. Nicholls is an economist with the U.S. Department of Agriculture. A graduate of Oberlin College, he has done graduate work in economics at Harvard University.

of income, for each year or time period, possessed by each earning unit in relation to the income of each other unit in society. The *median* measures the income halfway through the distribution, and the quintile identifies the amount of income received by each one-fifth of society from the lowest to the highest. Thus, one can determine that in 1935–36 the lowest quintile in the United States received 4% of the total income, while in 1962 the lowest fifth received 6%.[3] A comparison of patterns over time and of patterns between countries allows the generalization of comparisons and *trends* in income distribution.

Major decisions in the use of income distributions involve: 1. the type of income to be measured—product, personal, or disposable; 2. whether income is measured before or after taxes (a particularly important factor in dealing with the income received by the top five percent);[4] 3. whether income in kind (nonmoney income) is included, important especially in dealing with public services used by and intended for the poor, such as health and housing.

The *Lorenz curve* depicts graphically the distribution of income and wealth by arraying percentages of population against percentages of money as in the diagram below. This typical Lorenz

FIGURE 1. INEQUALITY OF WEALTH AND INCOME IN THE UNITED STATES.

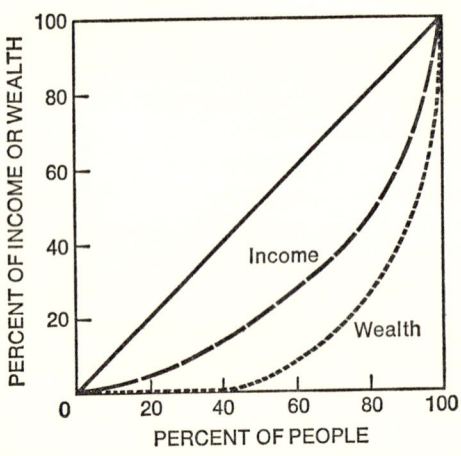

Source: Paul A. Samuelson, *Economics* (New York: McGraw-Hill Book Co., 8th edition, 1970), p. 112.

curve shows that the lowest 20% of the population received 5% of the income while the top 20% of the population receive 40% of the income. Wealth is typically less equally distributed than income, as we shall see later on in this chapter.

But for now, one important point should be noted about the study of social inequality. Inequality may take several forms, including income, wealth, and education; one way to measure inequality is to compare the total amount received by those getting the least of the good things with the amount received by an equal number receiving more. Such comparisons are commonly made by examining the share of income, wealth, education, and the like received by quintile groups.

MULTIDIMENSIONALITY OF INEQUALITY

Inequality in society is multidimensional; it is present in the distribution of many variables other than income. Such inequality also tends to perpetuate itself over time, through the interaction of the private market, family socialization and inheritance, and governmental policy.

For our purposes, seven dimensions of inequality may be identified (it is surely possible to find more), each of which are interrelated with income inequality, and each of which may be summarized by a distribution. The seven dimensions are:

1. Income
2. Wealth
3. Education
4. Services
5. Self-respect
6. Cognitive skill
7. Occupational status

Each of these dimensions will be described in terms of the magnitude of the inequality which characterizes it in contemporary American society.

INCOME

Income is the most commonly studied dimension of inequality in society. It tends to be less equally distributed than education and more equally distributed than wealth. Studies of income inequality in the United States find that the income distribution has changed very little over the past thirty years. The bottom fifth earn about 5% of the total income, and the top fifth receive about one-half the total income.

WEALTH

Wealth is generally defined as the value of assets or property; it includes stocks, bonds, savings, consumer durables, housing, and insurance. The Lorenz curve for wealth is strongly bowed toward the lower right corner, showing that ownership tends to be highly concentrated in the hands of the rich, with the upper 6% holding 57% of the wealth, and the top 56% holding 98% of the wealth.[5]

The top 6%, which hold 57% of the wealth, also control the decisions of almost all corporations as to what shall be invested. Indeed, the country's major corporations are owned in large part by a few hundred wealthy individuals.[6]

All individual components of wealth are unequally distributed between the rich and the poor, although homes, durables, and liquid assets are more equally distributed than investment.[7]

EDUCATION

Education is more equally distributed than income or wealth. When the amount of education received by each American is plotted by the number of persons receiving that amount of education, three peaks are found in the distribution: 14% at grade eight; 29% at grade twelve; and 8% at grade sixteen.[8] The economist Thurow has noted that "if the distribution of education determines the distribution of income, there should be a greater number of individuals concentrated at the center of the income range [than there actually are]."[9] But since there are more people who are very poor than those who have received very little education, we may conclude that poverty, in most cases, is accounted for by noneducational influences such as discrimination. In the upper ranges, on the other hand, the education and income distributions are more alike, suggesting the oft-heard assertion that education is a necessary but not sufficient condition for higher income.

SERVICES

Public education, to cite one prominent example, is only one of a long list of services provided to citizens in a "mixed economy" like that of contemporary America. Education is a *universally provided* service in that it is available to all citizens regardless of income. Universal services are organized in society where collective action is widely perceived to be more effective than allowing the mechanism of the free market to predominate. Education could, after all, be provided privately, with each family purchasing those educational services it required or could afford. However, the United States, like most modern societies, has chosen to provide education universally, viewing the opportunity to become educated as a sufficiently important social need that people should not be permitted to do without it.

Other services are provided *categorically* in the United States; that is, one has to qualify, generally by being able to demonstrate a need for the service. A whole variety of public-housing programs, for instance, have been established over the past thirty years to benefit low- and moderate-income families. These programs are *means-tested;* that is, a family must demonstrate that its income is beneath a certain level if it is to qualify for the service. Similarly, antipoverty programs have been directed only to areas and individuals who meet poverty standards; health programs have been established that are means-tested; and public day-care centers, legal services, and casework services have been made available only for those who can demonstrate a lack of income.

Despite a great expansion in categorical services for the poor and the near-poor in the 1960's, the United States still provides fewer health and housing services than most of the Western European societies in which the "welfare state" has been more fully developed.

Few services that are provided categorically to low-income persons in the United States are of sufficient quality to equal the services available on the private market to those who can afford them. The poor, for example, make one-third the number of dental visits as the nonpoor. They also have fewer doctors and other medical practitioners available to them. In the neighborhoods in which sanitation services tend to be less effective than in other parts of town, police protection is inadequate to restrain street crime, and few recreational areas, parks, and libraries are typically available. Public transportation is often inadequate, especially for the prospective inner-city worker who seeks to use it to commute to a suburban work place; when transportation is available publicly, its cost is often excessive for poor persons. Legal services are also difficult to acquire, and the quality of such service is often restricted by the demands made upon the community legal services or the public defender.

The case is made against the importance of services in reducing inequality by those who contend that the main beneficiaries of services are those who fill the jobs of service providers. To be sure, much that is called social service is simply talk—advice, referral, consultation—but an appropriate package of casework, housing, health, legal, and transportation services can directly benefit the poor by increasing the material well-being of the individual as well as his social adjustment, freeing whatever income he has to satisfy more enjoyable but less basic wants.

SELF-RESPECT

In an acquisitive society, self-respect tends to be distributed unequally and in direct relation to income. A long and complex debate exists among social scientists as to the reasons for the lower self-respect of the poor than the well-off, and the degree to which this factor is important in affecting behavior. Some, taking the "culture-of-poverty" position, argue that a low level of self-esteem is widely shared among the poor and prevents poor persons from taking advantage of economic and social opportunities that may be made available to them. Critics of the culture-of-poverty theory tend to stress the fact that the poor behave as they do because they have little money and little chance to make money and that their behavior would be not at all different from the rest of us if opportunities were provided them. Still a third position seeks to combine the first two, arguing that the experience of poverty is a pervasive one, but that the poor will respond to changes in their economic position and opportunity.[10]

COGNITIVE SKILL

Great controversy surrounds our knowledge of the ways in which cognitive skills are distributed in society. Such skill is usually measured by tests of aptitude, like the IQ test, which themselves are frequently criticized for what they omit and for biases they are alleged to contain. Christopher Jencks and associates conclude that cognitive skill is determined by many different factors, including heredity, total environment, economic status, amount and quality of schooling, and discrimination. They suggest that the first two factors, heredity and total environment, are the most powerful in affecting performance on tests.[11] There remains much to be learned about how test performance relates to occupational success, however, and the next few years will surely see rapid advances in our knowledge in this and related areas.

OCCUPATIONAL STATUS

The jobs that people hold in society are themselves subject to ranking, in terms of the income they produce, and the esteem and power they provide their holders. Much occupational status is passed on from generation to generation, as family socialization passes on traditions, skills, contacts, and expectations. In one sense, then, an occupation reflects the way in which an individual maintains both his own and his children's position in the structure of social inequality. A job reflects education, skills, and inherited wealth, and says much about the income, education, skill, wealth, and self-esteem a person's children are likely to possess, as we shall explore more fully later in this chapter.

MODELS FOR UNDERSTANDING INEQUALITY

In his classic work on American race relations, Gunnar Myrdal pointed to the workings of a "vicious circle" that served to perpetuate an inferior position for Black Americans in American society.

Myrdal posited a large number of variables in dynamic interaction with each other: prejudice, discrimination, employment, wages, housing, education, health, and the like. Further, he suggested, "any change in any one of these factors, independent of the way in which it is brought about, will, by the aggregate weight of the cumulative effects running back and forth between them all, start the whole system moving in one direction or another." [12] A similar relationship appears to exist among most of the variables examined in the section above.

For instance, people with higher incomes tend to own more capital and assets, and they tend to use the returns for reinvestment. This advantage is magnified and extended as they pass on to their own children, through inheritance, much of the wealth that they have accumulated.

The well-off also tend to use their wealth to support their children at the best educational institutions, whether secondary or college, thereby maximizing their investment in the "human capital" of their own children.

An analogous process exists among the middle classes, although there the transmittal of wealth is less dramatic. Middle-class family life tends to convey the values of work and success. Likewise, a general level of economic comfort contributes to the nurturance of the middle-class child.

For many of the poor, the vicious cycle works in the opposite direction. Low income means little or no accumulation of savings, the disruption of family ties, the questioning of education and mobility, and the inability of the parent to transmit to his and her children either security or employable skill.

Jencks and his associates have recently shown quite dramatically the limits of education in affecting income, wealth, and even cognitive skills. Challenging the traditional American view that education is a sure-fire method of reducing inequality, Jencks has argued:

> First, economic success, as measured by occupational status and income, depends on a variety of factors besides competence. Second, competence depends on many things besides basic cognitive skill. Third, standardized tests do not measure basic cognitive skill with complete accuracy. . . . Our research has convinced us not only that cognitive inequality does not explain economic inequality to any significant extent, but that educational inequality does not explain cognitive inequality to any significant extent. The amount of schooling an individual gets has some effect on his test performance, but the quality of his schooling makes extraordinarily little difference.[13]

However much the traditional view that formal education guarantees economic success will be reformulated in light of Jencks' findings, the fact remains that although education is more equally distributed than income, it is still quite unequally distributed. And Jencks notwithstanding, the fact remains that income, wealth, and services like education are *often* closely linked in American society, reducing the prospects of mobility from one class to another, and perpetuating many advantages for the financially secure from generation to generation. In education itself, Miller and Roby remind us, a chain of relations exists whereby low income leads to a low tax base, which leads to poor schools, which leads to less well-trained teachers, which leads to low income for students.[14]

The dimensions of inequality may be seen to relate to each other in a variety of ways, each suggesting a different explanation of inequality and a different method for reducing inequality. Let us look at four such hypothetical sets of relations or models. The first suggests that it is the distribution of education that is crucial, and that from it arises the distribution of skills which then leads to the distribution of wealth and income. This may be identified as the *cognitive model of inequality*. It is this model which has been subjected to recent criticism by Jencks. The way to reduce inequality, contend those who subscribe to this model, is to make education more widely available throughout society, thereby moving toward the equalization of skill and therefore income and wealth.

A second model begins with the distribution of income and posits that this distribution leads to the distribution of education and then to the distribution of occupational position. This model may be identified as the *transfer model*, for it suggests the policy of making additional income available to low-income persons, in order that they might afford more education. Again, however, education is at the heart of the model, and the faith is retained that through education, occupational position can be increased.

A third model posits the distribution of wealth as the key factor in producing the distribution of income and ultimately occupational status and achievement in society. Education, in this model, is only a secondary factor; what is important is the passing on from one generation to another of economic advantage. This may be identified as the *accumlated-wealth model* and it suggests a policy of inequality reduction of reform in the system of taxation, moving toward the equalization of wealth and income by directly requiring the sharing of inheritances and disparities in capital possession.

A fourth model stresses the primacy of governmental services and sees services as directly related to the self-respect of low-income persons, the development of their cognitive skills, and ultimately the jobs and education that they receive. This may be identified as the *service model* and it suggests that policy intervention take the form of an upgrading of the services available to low-income persons—such as health, housing, welfare, education, and the like.

In the opinion of the authors, the model that is most nearly correct in describing the pattern of inequality that prevails in the United States and the policy required to reduce that inequality is the third; that is, the one that places the distribution of wealth at the center of the stage. The distribution of wealth is highly unequal in American society, as Table I indicates.

TABLE I. DISTRIBUTION OF WEALTH: DECEMBER 31, 1962

Wealth	Consumer units* (in millions)	Percent Distribution Consumer units	Wealth
Total	57.9	100%	100%
Negative	1.0	2	*
Zero	4.7	8	*
$1–999	9.0	16	*
1,000–4,999	10.8	19	2
5,000–9,999	9.1	16	5
10,000–24,999	13.3	23	18
25,000–49,999	6.2	11	18
50,000–99,999	2.5	4	14
100,000–199,999	0.7	1	8
200,000–499,999	0.5	1	13
500,000+	0.2	*	22

* A "consumer unit" consists of a household (a family, or persons living singly).

Source: Herman Miller, *Rich Man, Poor Man*, Table IX-3, p. 157.

Ten percent of the population owns no wealth at all, and one-fourth of the population possesses less than $1,000 in total wealth. Moreover, 57% of the nation's wealth is owned by 6% of the population, and three-fourths of the nation's wealth is owned by 17% of the population. Wealth, it should be remembered, is not an inert quality, but can be transformed quite readily into disposable income, income that can keep a college student in school, provide superior child care and surroundings for youngsters, and cover emergency expenses for health and other exigencies.

Wealth not only is unequally distributed, but also directly related to income. Gabriel Kolko provides a table which shows that 93% of the total national net savings is owned by the highest 20% of the population on the income scale.[15] The bottom one-fifth holds minus 18% of the net savings, which means that they are in debt a whopping large amount.

The relation between income and occupation is perpetuated not only by the tendency of certain occupations to be more remunerative than others, but also by the tendency of this occupational advantage to be transferred intergenerationally. While the inheritance of status from father to son is by no means automatic, a child of high social-class background is three times more likely than a child of moderate social-class background to reach the highest decile of economic success, and over twenty-five times as likely as the child of the lowest social-class background.[16] To be sure, almost one-fourth of those who end up in the highest economic level have come from the bottom one-half of the social class ladder. Inequality is not absolute in American society; the lower the status of one's family of origin, and the lower its income and wealth, the lower the *probabilities* that one will achieve occupational status and income.

Relating to the basic model of "wealth leads to income leads to occupational status" are a variety of other relations, such as those between wealth and income, on the one hand, and education, on the other, and those between wealth and income, on the one hand, and self-respect, on the other. The lower one's income, the less likely that one has completed high school and college.

Table II shows that males earning less than $3,000 in 1970 had a median educational level of ten years of schooling, whereas males making $15,000 or more averaged 15.6 years of education. Numerous other studies have indicated that most varieties of mental illness are more prevalent among the poor than the rich.

It is often claimed that those who are well off have risen to the top because of their superior I.Q. However, Bowles and Gintis have shown that I.Q. is far less powerful than income or wealth in ex-

TABLE II. YEARS OF SCHOOL COMPLETED BY EMPLOYED MALES, 25–64, BY INCOME IN 1970

Males, 25–64	MSYC
$3,000	10.0
3,000–5,999	11.0
6,000–9,999	12.2
10,000–14,999	12.6
15,000+	15.6

Source: Table 7, *Current Population Reports: Population Characteristics*, Educational Attachment, March 1971 (altered for our use). The table is actually more complex, showing educational attainment for several income levels for high- and low-skill occupations.

plaining economic success. For a given level of social background and schooling, they show, differences in adult I.Q. add very little to the prediction of eventual economic success.[17] A person with an average number of years of schooling in an average socioeconomic family background, but with the highest level of cognitive skill, has a probability of 14.1% of attaining the highest economic success decile, an advantage of only 4 points over a person of average I.Q. The evidence is clear that it is not cognitive skill, as measured by I.Q. tests, that leads to economic success; rather it is the good fortune of having been born into a family of above average wealth and income.

INEQUALITY AND MOBILITY

The idea of "equality of opportunity" is a basic cultural norm in American society—how many times have you heard speakers refer to America's "egalitarian" society when they meant "equality of opportunity"? Despite the widespread acceptance of the norm, however, much inequality is structured into our society, and much of it is cumulative in form. People who rank low on one dimension tend to rank low on others. Thus, the question of social mobility is an important one to consider. Even if one's family of upbringing is at the bottom, what are his chances of making it into the upper positions of society?

There are a number of ways mobility occurs—one is through successful completion of high school or college. According to the consensus or functional theory, low-status children of high ability ought to be mobile, for they are needed to fill the positions their ability allows them to fill. However, in fact, many of these talented individuals are lost each year to further education: consider the implications of a situation in which students who rank between the 50th and 75th percentile on the aptitude level, and are poor, attend college at a rate of 48.2%, compared with the rate of 79.7% of their wealthier peers (who have incomes of $12,000 or above) at the same level of aptitude.[18] For those below the mean, the rich student is two-and-one-half times more likely than the poor student to attend college. Only if a student from a poor family ranks in the top 2% by national norms is he as likely as a wealthy student to go on to college. At least we have learned to "cream" the most able of the poor.

On the whole, sons tend to remain on the same socioeconomic level as their fathers. That is, mobility, upward or downward, tends to be the exception rather than the rule—thus dividing jobs into five major categories (elite 17%, middle-class 36%, skilled 19%, semiskilled 20%, and unskilled 8%). We find that in the United States the son of an elite father has three times the chance of the son of a middle-class father to become elite himself, and five times the chance of the son of a skilled worker. Further, he has sixteen times the chance of the semiskilled worker's son and eleven times the chance of the unskilled worker's son.[19]

The odds that a son of an elite will become a manual worker are one in seven. Indeed, the odds that a son of a middle-class worker will become a manual worker are one in five. For upward mobility, the odds are two in five that the skilled worker's son will become nonmanual, and one in five for the sons of the semiskilled and unskilled. Thus, typically, the odds are near four in five that you will end up in the same general type of work (manual, nonmanual) as your father. Over the past years, there has been more upward mobility than downward mobility, owing to the expansion of elite positions; how long this built-in trend toward "structural mobility" will continue is anybody's guess. However, compared with Great Britain, Japan, and the Netherlands, the United States has experienced relatively low amounts of downward mobility of elites, and about an average amount of upward mobility of manual workers.

Now, why is it that our class structure is so sticky? Why do so many children remain on the occupational ladder at about the same point as their parents? We suggest that these positions are inherited through such means as direct inheritance of wealth, direct inheritance of position, advantages of early socialization, availability of benign environment, association with similarly favored peers, expectations for behavior, positive self-image, quality of education, freedom from fear and insecurity, and the like. For the analysis of how these built-in factors of advantage and disadvantage work, sociologists have investigated quite closely the behavior of the major social classes in society, and the cultural systems in which they have developed.

CLASS AND CLASS CULTURE IN AMERICA

Thus far in this chapter we have largely talked about patterns of inequality; we can begin now to examine the consequences of such inequality for the behavior of members of different social classes. In discussing inequality to this point, we have talked in terms of individuals arrayed on the basis of their possession of differential access to life chances, such as income, education, wealth, and the like. Henceforth, when we talk of *class* we will speak of more than statistical categories of people.

Classes, in the Marxian sense, are categories of persons that share a common position vis-à-vis the relations of production, and come to share a common consciousness or ideology that interprets the world and guides their action.[20] In another sociological sense, that sense pioneered by Max Weber, classes may be seen as "status groups." Status groups, Weber noted, contain three components: a societal component—prestige or honor; a group component—a certain life-style; and an individual component—self-esteem. Status groups form around ideal interests in society, values such as religion, education, and they seek to realize these interests in social life. They may develop a life of their own, independent of classes in the Marxist sense.[21]

The tension between Weber and Marx is a basic one in the study of social class. For Marx, classes must reflect the relations of production; to Weber, classes may reflect other values in addition to economic ones. The concept of class subculture is useful in seeing the degree to which economic and other interests come to play a part in the way people behave in social classes. The term subculture reminds us that ties exist between this category and the larger society —in values, coercion, possible mobility, and the like.

We will use the term subculture to describe variants of contemporary American class styles and will suggest that five major class subcultures exist in the contemporary United States.

The idea of class subculture is a fashionable one these days, as we hear much about the Culture of Poverty, the Hard-hats, the Silent Majority, and Middle America. Presumably, class subcultures emerge from a basic aspect of structure in the class system, but they may also develop relatively enduring patterns of value and behavior. It is the task of the social scientist to cut through social mythology and give an accurate picture of those class subcultures that exist, often not an easy task in an era in which sociological analysis and public image-making are frequently closely related.

Consider the case of the so-called culture of poverty. Does it exist in actuality as a self-defeating behavioral complex adopted by the poor? Or, is it largely a fictional concept popularized in the press and other media, based on an inaccurate reading of sociological evidence? Now think about the working-class subculture, as popularized by Archie Bunker and his family. Is this an accurate image of the many millions of working-class Americans?

Sociologists have conducted a number of case studies of different class subcultures in American society. Among the leading studies are those of W. Lloyd Warner, Herbert Gans, Elliot Liebow, Ulf Hannerz, and John Seeley and associates (this last is actually a Canadian study).[22] Not all class cultures have been studied in detail, nor does the evidence from the studies so far done appear incontrovertible. However, a list of tentative findings (as in Table III below) may be useful in examining the different characteristics of different class cultures. The material in Table III shows that class subcultures *do* differ in a variety of important societal characteristics, such as

TABLE III. CLASSES AS SUBCULTURES: SELECTED CHARACTERISTICS

CLASS-TYPE	Child rearing	Family
LOWER CLASS	Variable, adult-centered and peer rels.	Often female based, much conflict.
WORKING CLASS	Adult-centered	Family circle basic. Sexual segregation. Extended relations.
LOWER-MIDDLE CLASS	Child-centered	More egalitarian Nuclear family. Home central.
UPPER-MIDDLE CLASS	Adult-directed	Egalitarian.
UPPER CLASS	Adult-directed	Woman's role formally patterned. Some personal eccentricity expected.

child rearing, family structure, neighboring, associational life, occupational orientation, and orientation toward education. One's chances of achieving wealth and income vary according to the class subculture in which one is raised. Class subcultures are adaptations to different situations of comfort and opportunity. As such, they are also channels for future occupational and social development.

Just what form the struggle to reduce inequality will take in future years is dependent at least in part on the basic orientations of

TABLE III. CLASSES AS SUBCULTURES: SELECTED CHARACTERISTICS

Neighboring	Associational	Occupational	Educational
Neighbors as threat, sporadic peer rels.	Little membership in formal orgs. Gangs, "social activity clubs" more common.	Transistory, absence of work identity. Turn to expressive life-styles.	Distrusted, seen as instrumental.
Strong peer society. Childhood friends.	Unions about all. Expressive skills basic. Intolerant of "differences."	Work a means to income.	Instrumental.
Very common.	Belong to those which support home values, orderliness.	Provides status.	Means to status.
Moderate.	High participation in instrumental groups. Often national or regional.	Centrality of career. Focus on job satisfaction.	End in self, as well as means.
Formal relations less common than LMC.	High participation. Also "society."	Idea of "calling." Family tradition.	End in self, part of "perfection" of individual.

American class culture. How do we perceive such important institutions as political parties, educational institutions, social-welfare institutions, and community organizations? How they present themselves and are received in the different class cultures obviously affects much of the response many Americans make toward the political and social action, if any, that we will choose. Class subcultures, in short, have served in American society largely to legitimate existing inequalities of wealth, income, and opportunity. But, under *certain* circumstances, explored elsewhere in this volume, classes may yet become organized in *this* country to serve as active agents for social change of inequality-reducing significance.

INEQUALITY IN COMPARATIVE PERSPECTIVE

Some perspective on the degree of equality we might strive to implement may be gained from an examination of inequality in comparative perspective. It is widely known, of course, that the world is divided into richer and poorer nations, and that the gap between the rich and the poor is apparently widening. Within each of the nations of the world, in addition, there also exist varying degrees of inequality, and this is what we shall examine in this section.

Three major facts should be recognized about comparative equality across nations: first, every nation goes through several distinct stages in the distribution of income in its historical economic development. Accordingly, the comparison of two nations or societies may be the comparison of different historic stages. Second, the developed societies clearly have less inequality than the underdeveloped ones, for capitalistic ownership may early mean self-perpetuation of traditional patterns of wealth. Third, advanced countries whose economy is developed may themselves vary widely in the degree of inequality.

Several stages of development of differences in inequality may be outlined: 1) *Preindustrial Society:* Here there tends to be a general equality of poverty, little wealth, and a traditional basis of economic activity in agriculture or primitive industry. 2) *Economic Dualism:* Here the growth of capitalism and industry occurs in what is essentially an agricultural society. A distinct inequality characterizes many underdeveloped societies in this stage. A large lower class exists and a high concentration of wealth exists in the upper positions, due to a high reward for past training of capitalists. Since the rich tend to invest in luxuries and low-utility goods, there tends to be capitalistic self-perpetuation of wealth.

3) *Take-Off:* At this point a broad-based population is needed to perform increasingly skilled tasks in the industrial economy. A process of equalization of income takes place along with urbanization and industrialization. Governments begin to assume some responsibility for the transfer of income from the wealthy to the deserving poor, and some services are provided universally as well

as categorically. The beginnings of a progressive tax system often develop at this stage. 4) *The Welfare State:* This stage, which has already been entered by societies such as the Netherlands, the United Kingdom, Sweden, and Denmark, and at whose portals the United States tends to dally, brings the welfare of individuals to the forefront of the societal agenda, taking precedence over the growth of income and production. Ideally, social services grow to meet social needs, caused by technological and social change.

Now, with this general summary of stages in the development of inequality, we can compare developed with underdeveloped societies, and, later, several developed capitalist with mixed economies, to see how the trends work in reality, and whether the stages are accurate predictors of reality.

Comparing a number of developed countries with a number of underdeveloped countries, we can see that the differences in the percentage of family income received by the lowest 60% of families does not differ greatly between the two groups.

TABLE IV. PERCENTAGE OF FAMILY INCOME RECEIVED BY THE LOWEST 60% OF POOREST FAMILIES

Underdeveloped Countries		*Developed Countries*	
India (1950)	28.5	United States (1950)	32.0
Ceylon (1952–3)	27.7	Gr. Britain (1951–2)	33.3
Lebanon (1960)	28.0	W. Germany (1950)	29.0
Mexico (1957)	21.2	Denmark (1952)	29.5
Colombia (1953)	31.4	Netherlands (1950)	29.5
Salvador (1946)	32.2		
Puerto Rico (1954)	30.3		

Source: Gannagé, E., "Distribution of Income in Underdeveloped Countries," p. 346, Table 6, in Marchal and Ducros (eds.), *The Distribution of National Income,* modified from Simon Kuznets, "Distribution of Income by Size," *Quantitative Aspects of the Growth of Nations,* VIII, *Economic Development and Cultural Change,* Vol. XI, No. 2, Part II, January, 1963, Table 3.

However, when the amount of income received by the upper 10% of the families is compared, it is clear that the pattern of inequality is greater in the underdeveloped than in the developed countries.

When we reach the third and fourth stages, however, and compare developed nations, we see very little difference in the percentage of pretax incomes that go to the top 20% and the lowest 60% in the mixed economies of Europe and the American economy. Recent research by Thurow and Lucas[23] leans toward the statistical finding of equality between the United States and West Germany, the United Kingdom, and Sweden, three mixed economies. In each of these countries, an 8-to-1 ratio was found between the average income of the richest quartile and the poorest quartile. One major exception to this ratio is Japan, which, astoundingly, has only a 5-to-1 rich–poor ratio in income, at the same time that it maintains the world's highest growth rate.

Most studies of comparative inequalities have focused on pretax income, thereby overlooking the greater tax and greater posttax equality that exists in Great Britain, as well as the greater redistribution of income through services that characterizes the Scandinavian societies like Sweden (where the poor have a higher absolute and relative share of services than in the United States).

In summary, then, comparative trends between rich and poor nations show a clear and predicted inequality (on the basis of our stages of inequality development) between the developed and less-developed world. While the more capitalistic society of the United States shows relative pretax equality in relation to the welfare states of Western Europe, it shows clearly greater inequality than capitalist Japan. Moreover, the welfare states are still young and they may show greater equality than the United States later in this century.

TRENDS IN EQUALITY IN THE UNITED STATES

The United States, as we have seen, is not an egalitarian society; on the other hand, neither is it a society in which mobility from generation to generation, both up and down, is unknown. Rather, the United States appears to be a society of rather large inequality with rather large amounts of social mobility. The purpose of this section is to examine trends in the development of inequality in the United States in recent years. The answer appears to be that in most cases inequality has been slightly reduced over the past few decades, but only slightly. As Jencks summarizes it:

> The basic trends are almost certainly real, however. There seems to have been some reduction in income inequality during the Depression, and there seems to have been a further reduction during World War II. The

degree of inequality did not change much from 1946–1960. There was a slight decline in inequality from 1960 to 1968 and a reversal of the 1960–1968 trend between 1968 and 1970.

The major conclusion to be drawn from this data seems to be that it takes a cataclysm like the Great Depression or World War II to alter the distribution of income significantly.[24]

TABLE V. PRETAX INCOMES OF FAMILIES AND INDIVIDUALS IN EACH QUINTILE AS A PERCENTAGE OF NATIONAL MEAN: 1929–1970

	1929	1935–1936	1941	1946	1960	1968	1970
Poorest Fifth	20	21	21	25	25	29	28
Fourth Fifth	45	46	48	56	55	57	55
Middle Fifth	70	71	77	80	80	80	79
Second Fifth	95	105	112	109	115	115	115
Top Fifth	270	259	244	231	225	218	223
Top 5 Percent	600	530	480	426	400	334	344
Mean (Current Dollars)	$2,340	$1,630	$2,210	$3,940	$6,820	$8,840	$10,100
(1968 Dollars)	$5,210	$4,340	$5,380	$6,620	$7,860	$8,840	$9,040

Source: Jencks, *Inequality*, p. 210.

Table V shows that as of 1970 the average income received by a family in the top 5% of the income distribution is twelve times higher than the average income of a family in the poorest fifth. A family in the poorest fifth receives slightly more than one-fourth the average income in society, whereas a family in the top fifth receives three-and-one-half times the societal average. Since 1929, however, it has been the top fifth whose relative income has dropped in relation to the poorest fifth. Nonetheless, since everyone's income has risen during that period, the absolute gap in dollars between the rich and the poor has increased. Thus, although the incomes of the rich rise at a slower rate than the incomes of the poor, in actual dollar terms, the added money received by the well-off every year far exceeds the additions to the income of the poor. A 5% raise to a man making $20,000 a year is larger than a 25% raise for one making $3,000 a year.

If we look into the crystal ball and try to predict future distributions of income in the United States, we are, of course, engaging in a risky business. The possibility of moderate or sweeping institutional, technological, economic, and demographic change makes an extrapolation exactly what it is—the extension of a trend on the basis of hunches and guesses. Extrapolation, therefore, should be interpreted with caution. With that warning in mind, we have projected the trends of the last ten years ahead to the year 2000. We have seen a mild equalization in income distribution for that period between 1960 and 1970. This distribution has become somewhat more equal for individuals not living in families than for families. The share of the top 5% for both families and unrelated individuals also indictates greater inequality. We estimate that, should current trends continue, the share of the lower fifth will be 8.1% of the total income by the year 2000 (up from 5.0%) and the share of the upper fifth will be down to 37.8% (down from 42.0%). These trends are extrapolated with the caveat

that policies continue to be made in the same areas and directions as in the 1960's;
that employment and population trends remain the same;
that technological advances and demand for labor grow in the same direction and at similar rates;
that the institutional framework remain similar.

The direction taken by all or a combination of the following attitudes and policies will have an effect on our estimate. The estimates we made above would be low

if there is a large shift of expenditures toward education and services;
if the income distribution and definition of income begin to include services;
if the institutions change so that the government owns more property and takes a more active role in training the handicapped and unemployed;
if the private sector dominates less and gives more employment opportunities to the poor; and, finally,
if the government decides to tax the income and the wealth of the rich at steeper rates.

On the other hand, this upward trend will probably be far less steep than our estimate

if the trend toward more help in education, services, and training is abandoned or not increased at the same rate;
if transfers to the poor and disabled are allowed to fall further behind the growth of other incomes;
if demand shifts further away from unskilled labor;

if government, as an employer, doesn't fill this gap, leaving a mass of undereducated hard-to-employ; and

if the American people and the political establishment can't see fit to change the distribution of income.

The choice of the amount of inequality we will have by the year 2000—for it is rather likely that social inequality will persist to some degree—is a choice that will be made in the legislative halls and in the streets and the polling places of the United States. It is an ongoing political decision, but one that, as we have seen, is highly susceptible to fundamental crises and changes in direction in society. Above all, the choice of how much inequality a society shall have is a *political* decision, and not a function of impersonal economic forces.

This book is an introduction to fresh and provocative ways in which that decision could be made in the years immediately ahead. The decision of just how much inequality of what variety we are to possess or tolerate is a decision that each of us makes in our roles as citizens—and in our capacity as caring and concerned beings. The choice is ours—between callous competition and the development of new forms of cooperation. The latter will require social change and experimentation toward the implementation of new ideologies and structures. New futures can be ours . . . if we dare.

1. S. M. Miller and Pamela Roby, *The Future of Inequality* (New York: Basic Books, 1970), p. viii.

2. Simon Kuznets, "Distribution of Income by Size," *Quantitative Aspects of the growth of Nations*, VIII, *Economic Development and Cultural Change*, Vol. XI, Number 2, Part II (January 1963), p. 1.

3. Herman Miller, *Income Distribution in the U.S.*, Bureau of the Census, 1960 Monograph (Washington: Government Printing Office, 1966), Table I-1, p. 3.

4. Herman Miller, *Rich Man, Poor Man* (New York: Thomas Crowell and Co., 1971), Table III-2, p. 29.

5. *Ibid.*, Table IX-3, p. 157.

6. William Domhoff, *The Higher Circles: The Governing Class in America* (New York: Random House, 1970).

7. E. C. Budd (ed.), *Inequality and Poverty* (New York: W. W. Norton, 1967), pp. 87–90.

8. Lester C. Thurow, *Poverty and Discrimination* (Washington, D.C.: The Brookings Institution, 1969), p. 68.

9. *Ibid.,* p. 67.

10. Cf. Sally Bould Van Til and Jon Van Til, "The Lower Class and the Future of Inequality," *Growth and Change* (January 1973), pp. 10–16.

11. Christopher Jencks et al., *Inequality: A Reassessment of the Effect of Family and Schooling in America* (New York: Basic Books, 1972).

12. Gunnar Myrdal, *An American Dilemma: The Negro Problem and Modern Democracy* (New York: Harper and Row, 1944), p. 1067.

13. Jencks, *Inequality,* p. 109.

14. Miller and Roby, *The Future of Inequality,* p. 122.

15. Gabriel Kolko, *Wealth and Power in America: An Analysis of Social Class and Income Distribution* (New York: Praeger, 1962), p. 48.

16. Samuel Bowles and Herbert Gintis, "I.Q. in the U.S. Class Structure," *Social Policy,* Vol. 3 (January–February 1973), Table 6, p. 73.

17. *Ibid.,* pp. 65–96.

18. Miller and Roby, *The Future of Inequality,* p. 125.

19. Thomas Fox and S. M. Miller, "Intra-Country Variations: Occupational Stratification and Mobility," in Reinhard Bendix and S. M. Lipset, eds., *Class, Status, and Power* (New York: The Free Press, 1966), pp. 574–76.

20. For an excellent presentation of this position, see T. B. Bottomore, *Classes in Modern Society* (New York: Vintage Books, 1966).

21. For an excellent presentation of this position, see S. M. Miller, *Max Weber* (New York: Thomas Y. Crowell Company, 1963).

22. Herbert Gans, *The Urban Villagers; Group and Class Life of Italian-Americans* (New York: Free Press of Glencoe, 1962).

Ulf Hannerz, *Soulside; Inquiries into Ghetto Culture and Community* (New York: Columbia University Press, 1970).

Elliot Liebow, *Tally's Corner; A Study of Negro Streetcorner Men* (Boston: Little, Brown, 1967).

John Seeley, *Crestwood Heights; A Study of the Culture of Suburban Life* (New York: Basic Books, 1956).

W. Lloyd Warner, *Democracy in Jonesville, A Study in Quality and Inequality* (New York: Harper, 1949).

———, (ed.), *Yankee City* (New Haven: Yale University Press, 1963).

23. L. C. Thurow and Robert E. Lucas, "The American Distribution of Income: A Structural Problem," study prepared for use by the Joint Economic Committee, March 17, 1972.

24. Jencks, *Inequality,* pp. 209–10.

II. NEW PERSPECTIVES ON INEQUALITY IN AMERICA

3
Traditional Views: Liberalism and Conservatism

Jon Van Til

Certainly the two most common historic ideologies regarding inequality have been conservatism and liberalism. Conservatives have tended to take the functional approach toward the study and evaluation of inequality, as outlined in Chapter 1. That is, they examine the contributions inequality makes to an ongoing economy and society. Liberals, on the other hand, have generally adopted a watered-down version of conflict theory in evaluating and studying inequality. That is, they have focused on the ways in which inequality reflects a group struggle for the good things of life. However, liberals have tended to go less far in developing the ramifications of their conflict theory than the two perspectives examined in detail in this section, populism and socialism.

The issues that separate conservatives and liberals were well delineated in the last book of a well-known economist.[1] Summing up the pros and cons of inequality, the late Clair Wilcox noted that, in a market economy, production can be seen as guided by the dollar votes of consumers. That is, each of us can be seen as translating our incomes into votes for the production and consumption of material goods. When these votes are distributed unequally, productive resources may well be allocated efficiently. However, inequality will be in likelihood resented by those whose incomes are low, giving rise to social unrest and political disorder. Such unrest is more likely when those with higher incomes cannot demonstrate that their incomes have been earned. Wilcox noted: "Incomes can be regarded as earned if they have been received in payment for the performance of a socially useful service and if they have been determined in a competitive market. There are many large incomes that can be justified in this way. But there are others that cannot."[2]

Wilcox then turns to an examination of the origins of great fortunes to see the basis upon which they were built. He notes that most of them were built upon the appropriation of natural resources, or rising land values, or the enjoyment of special privileges, or the profits of monopolies, or the practice of financial manipulation. Quoting Wilcox:

> None of these is to be justified as earned.
>
> A person who cuts down virgin timber, digs up minerals, or releases oil and gas for shipment to market is clearly entitled to a return for his labor. But the person who first took possession of these resources, paying little or nothing for them, and then sold them, did not earn the money that he made. He was not responsible for the existence of the resources. He did not plant the trees. He did not put the minerals in the ground. He did not create the reservoir of oil or gas. He simply converted nature's gifts to all mankind into a fortune for himself.[3]

Wilcox also finds those who build fortunes on increases in land value to be building fortunes on an unearned base. He distinguishes between these unearned fortunes and the earned income of those who provide services that are "obviously in demand."[4] He also notes that "Great fortunes, whatever their origin, may be perpetuated through the rights of bequest and inheritance."[5] He notes that taxation has not gone far toward the abolition of inheritance.

What, then, is the defense for private riches? Wilcox summarizes a number of conservative arguments:

1. It is said that rich people perform a useful function when they spend their money, since their expenditures a) provide other people with employment; b) make other people envious, thus giving them an incentive to work and save; and c) promote culture, establishing and maintaining higher values for the rest of the community to imitate.
2. It is said that the rich perform a useful function when they save their money, thus providing the economy with capital.
3. It is said that they perform a useful function when they give their money away, financing great foundations, universities, and other worthy undertakings.[6]

Wilcox finds these attempted justifications, "partly fallacious, partly exaggerated, partly true."[7] The self-indulgence of the rich is not necessary to provide the rest of us with jobs, and as an incentive to work and saving, inequality need not be extreme. Further, many of the rich do not give their money away in benefaction. Thus, Wilcox concludes, the extreme conservative position must be rejected: "Extreme inequality is unnecessary. It is also socially undesirable. It perverts social values—establishes materialistic standards to guide behavior. It denies to those with lower incomes an equal opportunity to participate in the life of the community, robbing them of their self-respect. It makes for bitterness and antagonism among the poor, and for callousness and arrogance among the rich. It obstructs the development of social morality. It divides the nation into contending groups. It checks the free flow of sympathy and hinders action for the common good. We should be better off without it." [8]

But if extreme inequality is rejected, limited inequality is not. "Does it follow that society would be better served by precise equality? There are considerations that compel a negative reply." [9] Inequality, Wilcox tells us, has its uses. First, it is an incentive, indeed, the major incentive for productive effort. "Unequal wages persuade men to work harder. Unequal profits promote managerial efficiency. The lure of larger incomes stimulates invention, innovation, and technical progress. Other incentives could be used: differences in leisure, titles, decorations, and other symbols of prestige. But these would be as open to criticism as are differences in income. And they would be more difficult to administer. Pecuniary motivation is both effective and convenient." [10]

Secondly, "inequality promotes the proper allocation of scarce resources among competing uses. Some goods are more wanted than others. To obtain them, consumers will pay a higher price. Those who produce them will command labor by paying a higher wage. Industries which satisfy growing demands will expand. Those whose products are less wanted will decline." Therefore, social change can be "effected without compulsion. It will be brought about by differences in prices and in incomes." [11] In clear form, Wilcox thus presents the liberal statement that justifies limited inequality. Inequality is first an incentive and secondly a noncoercive allocator of scarce resources. With the latter argument, Wilcox joins forces with those liberal economists that can be traced back to Adam Smith. The market mechanism is seen as noncompulsive, based only on the preferences of human beings. Both the populists and the socialists take exception to this contention, claiming that the market mechanism itself is a most compulsive human institution.

Wilcox, on the other hand, contends that a society which abandons inequality will be compelled to adopt one of two undesirable alternatives. Either it will have to coerce consumers or it will have to coerce labor. The coercion of consumers forces people to go without things that they want and take things that they do not want. The coercion of workers, on the other hand, is purchased at the cost of liberty. Thus, Wilcox concludes, "Of the possible methods of accomplishing the allocation of resources among competing uses, variation in income appears to be the most desirable." [12] He concludes his discussion by noting that absolute equality requires state control. We quote in entirety:

> If it tried hard enough, a government might succeed in making incomes equal. But it would have to employ stern measures to do so. Since private enterprise would result in differences in profit, the government would have to forbid it. Since private saving would yield different amounts of interest, the government would have to prohibit accumulation of capital by anyone but the state. Since private employment would involve differences in wages, the government would have to make every workman an employee of the state. The implication of such measures must be plain. Exact equality is not to be obtained in a market economy. It would require the public ownership and operation of all industry and the concentration of economic authority in the hands of the state.[13]

As a defender of the market economy of mature capitalist societies, Wilcox is forced to reject the more radical egalitarian perspective of socialism for the limited inequality of enlightened liberal capitalism, as reinforced with the various mechanisms of the welfare state. The debate between liberals and conservatives on inequality, then, centers largely on the degree to which the government will intervene, always within limits, on the distributive mechanisms involved in the market and the inheritance of wealth. Both liberals and conservatives agree that the market mechanisms must be central to society. Conservatives urge a hands-off policy by government on both inheritance and the accumulation of wealth and income, tending to accept what the market yields. Liberals, on the other hand, call for intervention, but always limit that intervention so as not to displace the basic functioning of the market.

In recent years, however, even a Republican President such as Richard Nixon has felt compelled to regulate market proceedings quite closely in order to restrain inflationary pressures within the economy. Two ideological perspectives long present in American society as minority perspectives developed new strength in the 1960's and the 1970's in light of the economic and social turmoil of those decades. These perspectives, socialism and populism, are described in some length in the following two chapters. They are presented here not because they are dominant in the thinking of Americans, but rather because they provide alternative perspectives on inequality that give promise of breaking the long and dreary theoretical and practical deadlock between liberals and conservatives on this issue.

Populists and socialists alike are in agreement that more forthright measures are required to reduce and restrain the pressures of inequality in contemporary America. Neither pespective is dedicated to the preservation of the market structure of the capitalistic system, although the populists tend to be far more comfortable with it than the socialists. Both perspectives raise correctly the question of the necessity of inequality, that necessity accepted by both liberals and conservatives.

As fresh and vigorous perspectives on the subject, and because they have been so long relegated to a couple of pages in texts on inequality, we feature populism and socialism in our account and treat conservatism and liberalism only skeletally. In this way we hope to take a small step toward righting an imbalance in the study of inequality. The perspectives we describe may not be implemented in whole or even in part in the next decade. But they are perspectives that challenge existing ways of thought and suggest solutions to problems that both liberals and conservatives have long ago decided could be ignored. We offer the next two chapters, then, as challenges to the conventional wisdom of the last century of American social and economic thought. Whether these ideologies will remain more than minority perspectives is another of those decisions in which all of us will play a part by our action and inaction in the coming decade.

1. Clair Wilcox, *Toward Social Welfare* (Homewood, Illinois: Richard D. Irwin, Inc., 1969).
2. *Ibid.*, p. 17.
3. *Ibid.*, p. 18.
4. *Ibid.*, p. 17.
5. *Ibid.*, p. 20.
6. *Ibid.*, p. 21.

7. *Ibid.*
8. *Ibid.,* p. 22.
9. *Ibid.*
10. *Ibid.,* pp. 22–23.
11. *Ibid.,* p. 23.
12. *Ibid.*
13. *Ibid.*

4
The New Populism and America's Old Inequalities

Arthur B. Shostak

> *"What this country needs is a 'New Populism.' We need a 'positive coalition' to bring the hardhats and the students, and Americans everywhere—black, white, red and yellow, together again."*
>
> Senator Fred Harris
> (D., Oklahoma)

> *". . . while a new populism will not mean Nirvana or the Final Triumph of Virtue, it can make life a little more humane for a majority of our countrymen. Nothing more. But nothing less either."*
>
> Jack Newfeld and Jeff Greenfield
> *A Populist Manifesto* (1972), p. 222

Few recent developments on the American political scene have been as meteoric—and remain as unresolved—as the emergence of the New Populism. Uncompromising and sweeping in its dedication to radical social change, populism has overnight become *the* major American political movement to be based on social class rather than on race or culture contentions. As such, and despite its striking 1972 electoral setback in the McGovern defeat, the New Populism remains a major contender for lasting political significance (it already outdistances its only rivals on the Left, such as the women's liberation movement, some form of democratic socialism, and activist components in the youth or counterculture movement).

The overnight prominence of the New Populism was neither predictable nor entirely preventable, as it took both a remarkable pendulumlike swing in grass-roots styles of political in-fighting and in "ivory tower" scholarship to help resolve the matter. And this, despite a very old and stable place for populism in American history. . . .

Possibly two hundred years old as a native American tradition, populism reaches back to the radical political values of Samuel Adams, Thomas Jefferson, and Tom Paine; to Andrew Jackson, the muckrakers, sociologist Lester Frank Ward, and social critic Thorsten Veblen; to senators George Norris and Robert La Follette; and, partially, to presidents Franklin Delano Roosevelt and Harry S. Truman. It was plainly evident when the CIO was being formed, and made itself felt more recently in the dramatic 1973 win of rank-and-file reformers inside the United Mine Workers Union. It is especially compelling today in the recent campaigns and ideas of the late Martin Luther King, Jr., and Robert Kennedy, as well as in the contemporary efforts of Ralph Nader, John Gardner and his Common Cause Movement; senators Hart, Harris, Proxmire, and Kennedy; Father James Groppi, Father Geno Baroni, and many others of comparable verve and idealistic persuasion.

As recently, however, as the somnambulistic 1950's (the so-called End of Ideology decade), populism was ridiculed as a throwback to agrarian fantasies of the late 1800's—at best—and as a progenitor of nativistic fascism at worst. Certain excitable and nervous commentators (academics and journalists alike) judged it "paranoid," anti-intellectual, irrelevant, and even hopelessly romantic. Considered a rear-guard and even "redneck" movement, it was thought especially rooted in the status anxieties of a declining class, the petty bourgeosie. While it might continue to manifest itself in such reactionary forms as Birchism and Goldwaterism, it could hardly be regarded as a serious component in our national future.

At the same time, however, and more especially, on into the mid-1960's, the antagonizing scent of "tame the trusts!" and "soak the rich!" began to waft anew in the political air. Despite thirty years of alleged nationwide "affluence," and a premature declaration of the middle-class absorption of the working class (*embourgeoisefication*), large numbers of dissatisfied Americans began to raise impolite and culture-quaking questions: "Who owns the wealth? Who holds the power? And by what right? And, if the concentration of wealth and power should prove illegitimate, how might we redistribute both?" Related attitudes included distrust of public officials and a growing credibility gap; cynicism about the good faith of those in positions of great political and economic power; resentment against the elites that C. Wright Mills exposed; and a gnawing conviction that too many things in life are "fixed." To this many job-trapped Americans added the enervating experience of boredom at work and powerlessness just about everywhere else. Large numbers so impaled began to rediscover the New Populism.

Not surprisingly, the poll-sensitive politicians—and certain "ear-to-the-ground" academics—were close behind. A grass-roots rebellion in 1972 against the Democratic Party "establishment" gave rise to the McGovern and Wallace candidacies, and senators Reuben Askew, Fred Harris, Henry Howell, and others joined the populist ranks as well. Together they dedicated their (ill-starred) political fortunes to the (premature?) notion that a political majority could be built of both low- *and* moderate-income types, of whites and blacks, of hard-hats and long-hairs; or, if you will, of "Lionel," "Archie," "Mike," and "the boys at Kelsey's," in one powerful alliance.

At the same time, back at the Ivory Tower, historians like professors Pollack, Nugent, Rogin, Lasch, and others labored to make the New Populism intellectually respectable again. In their revisionist academic view, it became represented as a genuinely radical (and *not* rear-guard) movement with a radical social-change program. Neither nativist nor anti-Semitic by definition, revived populism was hailed as having come closer to the country's mood in the '68–'72 period than was ever true of the New Left. Accordingly, a close student of American politics, Professor Christopher Lasch, warned in 1972 that "if radicals and intellectuals adopt toward this movement an attitude of superior disdain, they will show that they have not only learned nothing from their recent experiences, but are probably determined to remain ignorant." [1]

As explained since, in the outstanding new book of its kind, *A Populist Manifesto: The Making of a New Majority*, by Jack Newfeld and Jeff Greenfield, the New Populism appeals to those who are tired of ideological wrangles and prefer to see theoretical niceties and hair-splitting subordinated to practical and potent immediate results. It seeks to "return to American politics the economic passions jettisoned a generation ago," and speaks to concrete economic interests of the have-nots. Overall, it takes as a goal nothing less than the total redistribution of privilege in America: "Some institutions and people have too much money and power, most people have too little, and the first priority of politics must be to redress that imbalance." [2]

CONCRETE ISSUES AND PROPOSALS

A critical plank in the New Populist platform demands radical restructuring of all of our tax laws. Particulars include the idea that we soon

close all tax loopholes, especially as benefit the rich and the corporations;
tax all church and foundation property incomes;
end the oil and gas depletion allowance;
greatly increase the taxes of the super-rich on inheritances, property, estates, stock transfers, and bank and insurance company assets (a 90% tax on inheritance is envisioned here); and
greatly decrease taxes on "the policeman from Queens and the dockworker from Brooklyn, because only on fairness can we build a new majority for justice." [3]

A second preoccupation is with gaining public control over private giant corporations: We are urged to

ban all mergers by any of the five hundred largest corporations;
break up all existing industrial oligopolies;
put in jail the key executives of companies that break antitrust laws and pollute the environment;
reinvigorate the Federal regulatory agencies;
create a separate court to try business crimes committed in regulated industries; and
promote union participation in management to democratize decision making and make sure profits are not the only corporate value.

Along with these reforms, populists call for public ownership of utilities (as did their forerunners in 1892), cable TV franchises for minorities, sweeping land-reform measures, and strict controls on all bank projects.

In the area of redistributing income downward the New Populists recommend

expansion of Social Security;
lowering of property and sales taxes;
vesting of pension rights;
free medical care for all; and

legislation requiring banks to invest some of their funds in declining neighborhoods.

Moreover, it is thought that breaking up monopolies in auto, steel, drugs, foodstuffs, and other basic industries would lower prices—thus redistributing income from the shareholders of concentrated industries to the consumer. This same contention is made concerning telephone and electric companies that, it is charged, bilk the average family out of thousands of dollars over a working lifetime.

Deeply concerned to promote what is just and worthy in the anguished and urgent call from "Archie Bunker" and his friends for "law and order" in the city, the two authors of the *Populist Manifesto* recommend

institution of strict gun controls;
an end to police corruption and bureaucracy;
penal reform that will emphasize rehabilitation instead of custody; and
an end to "police practices that hinder the work of deterrence."

Over and again the populist reformers come back to the gut-level issue of citizen powerlessness:

. . . placing working people on corporate boards would direct profits into increased job safety; expanding directorships of banks would provide loans to salvage urban neighborhoods; decisions on safety, or on pollution, would not be confined to automotive engineers and shareholders; the destruction of low-income communities for the real-estate expansion of Harvard or Columbia would be combated by neighborhoods with some power over their destiny.[4]

Accordingly, the preferred answer to "hard-hat" demands is thought available in the radical structural redistribution of political power. And this, in turn, will be based on recognition of the populist contention that "law and order" is a *real* issue for powerless, terrorized urbanites (of *both* races), and is not simply a slogan of demagogues, racists, and proto-fascists. Change here is predicated by the populists not on moralistic or humanitarian grounds, but on hardheaded self-interest ("the only antidote, the only thing deeper than fear. . .").

A sympathetic commentator notes that still other populist reforms not mentioned by Newfeld and Greenfield readily come to mind:

public financing of political campaigns;
federal chartering of corporations; and
public or cooperative ownership of industries other than utilities. . . .

The general objective, however, is clear: "To change our political and economic system from one that further enriches the rich and powerful to one that responds to the less-than-rich and not-so-powerful."[5]

AND NOW, A WORD FROM THE CRITICS...

For one thing, they make a lot of the narrow range of the New Populist concerns, including avoidance of the legitimate grievances of Blacks and the women's movement. The critics also stress the absence of concern for civil liberties, housing, education, mass transportation, ecology, and disarmament. For their part, while vaguely conceding that a New Populist movement must acknowledge such issues and groups if it is to be "authentic," Newfeld and Greenfield crisply and sarcastically insist that "this is a manifesto designed to move us closer toward justice, not Shangri-la."

A second criticism insists that the only real gainer here is likely to be George Wallace or men of his ilk. Much is made of the fact that economic populism has typically been linked with cultural nativism and racism. And there is no gainsaying the many distasteful ramifications in the past of populism in the form of rancid anti-intellectualism, rabid racism, and rear-guard hostility toward Catholics and Jews. Preoccupied with the know-nothing tendencies of nineteenth- and early twentieth-century populists, certain nervous critics discourage any resurgence of this plebian "redneck" tradition.

Newfeld and Greenfield range widely across time and politics in their own defense. They insist, for one thing, that the racist and religious demagoguery linked to old-line populism was never an authentic historical form of this political approach. For one of its authentic major tenets has always held that *all* the have-nots should unite against their common exploiters. Coming closer to home, they adroitly contend that with ersatz populists like Wallace already a factor in American politics, the development of a more cosmopolitan and unifying populist consciousness, far from being a spur to baser impulses, is probably a strategic antidote.

Far more telling is a third type of criticism, which contends that the superficial boldness of the New Populism turns out, on a close and exacting inspection, to be merely an evasion. The program is thought especially weak exactly where it claims its greatest strength, in the central matter of the distribution of income and power. Populists call for increasing taxes on the rich as if this would really help the poor, but many of the latter do not pay taxes now, and so will profit little from tax-law changes. To improve their lot there would have to be direct money transfers—a guaranteed annual income, or something similar to it. But, as Harvard political scientist James Q. Wilson caustically notes, Newfeld and Greenfield are silent on this: "Any discussion of income redistribution would divide the voters to whom they appeal, for those workers who do pay taxes are often opposed to giving money to those who do not." [6]

Sensitive to this charge, the two populist authors angrily reject it in its very entirety. For one thing, they insist (in a noncitation fashion) that between 1969 and 1971, welfare payments to white neighborhoods increased 60% faster than those to most black and Puerto Rican communities: this, a measure, in large part, of the growing inability of white adults to maintain the tradition of supporting their elderly parents without government subsidies. Ergo, it follows that white ethnics may be increasingly sympathetic to welfare reforms, and might be ready even now to support a guaranteed income or the like as a part of a New Populist platform. Similarly, much is made of the alleged fact that certain black leaders, including Rev. Jackson, State Senator Julian Bond, and congressmen Ron Dellums and John Conyers, are urging a populist alliance of low-income Blacks with low-income Whites, even while the shrill voices of ardent black separatists seem to be diminishing.

To be sure, forging alliances between black and white have-nots is no easy or sure matter. But the New Populists believe they have an edge in their hard-nosed realism, in their arm's-length insistence that Blacks and almost-poor Whites do not have to love or even like each other to forge a coldly rational alliance of straightforward self-interest. Rather, the task is one of reeducating adults and helping them secure a new and radical consciousness of American realities:

> If white and black communication workers find wages and promotions inadequate, whom should they blame? Each other? Or the conglomerate ITT that turned a profit of $350 million in 1970, and paid its board chairman, Harold Geneen, an unusual compensation of $766,000 (which is more than most Americans earn in a lifetime?)

> If white and black families are forced to compete against each other for decent housing at a fair price, whom should they blame? Each other? Or banks and insurance companies that finance a glut of new office buildings and luxury apartments and allow realty interests to make a profit out of slum housing? [7]

Once cemented, this pact between the have-nots is thought potentially significant enough to totally transform American politics—and, in collaboration with young voters and consumer, environment, and liberation supporters, enable the New Populists to take power.

However that may be, populists do not come back nearly as readily or as dramatically from a fourth, final, and especially telling criticism. Commentators take unnerving aim here at a New Populist preoccupation with economic explanations that is intrinsic to all radical political approaches. As social historian Christopher Lasch explains, because the New Populism treats politics as a reflection of economic self-interest, it has always found it difficult to explain the many subtle and vital connections between politics and culture. To understand these connections requires a theory of social class and an understanding of the way in which class interests, which seldom present themselves directly in economic form, are mediated by culture, which in turn acquires a life independent of its social origin.

Racism, for example, no longer has a clear basis in economic self-interest, even though it once furnished a rationale for slavery and other forms of exploitation. As racism nevertheless survives as a powerful force in American society, it cannot be eliminated simply by a more equitable distribution of goods (however much the New Populists might want to believe this!). Similarly, the Populist call for an equalization of educational opportunity as an antiracism move flounders on its own narrow quantitative approach, viz., more spending on schools, etc. Fatally overlooked are central cultural questions that boldly ask if compulsory schooling is inherently biased in favor of existing class structures, or if there is some relation between the monopoly that schools now have in education and the declining education content of work, leisure, and culture? [8]

Challenged in this way, the New Populist authors seem to waver between counterattack and apologetics. On the one hand, they insist that their preoccupation with economic determinism is well warranted:

We Americans are infested with the proposition that the rules of the game are not fair, that the fight is fixed; that the key to success in America is power, and that the key to power is the hidden angle, the fix, the money.[9]

On the other hand, the populists point out that at no time have they claimed to have all the answers.

In a time when politics offers the rhetoric

of redemption and revolution at the drop of a press release, we emphasize the limits of a political effort. This is not a summons to Utopia. It is not a call to revolution. We are talking instead about what is possible in this generation, in our time. . . .[10]

At their most defensive the authors concede that a total victory for the populist cause will only begin a long and unclear series of social gains. While a New Populism will not mean Nirvana or the Final Triumph of Virtue, it *can* begin to reverse the steady loss of faith and trust that afflicts our society—and that is no small thing.

Tried and found wanting in the 1973 McGovern debacle, the New Populism hovers about the scene waiting a 1976 comeback. Likely to be part of a Democratic Party onslaught against the social costs of the Nixon abandonment of "Great Society" designs, this plebian political ethos may peculiarly fit a pent-up need at Bicentennial time for a new and fresh political coalition, or a combination of the traditional liberalism of intellectuals and radical minorities, the new voting strength of the young (sixteen million new eighteen-year-old voters will be eligible in 1976), and the gnawing economic concerns of labor unions and white ethnic Americans. (A critic petulantly notes, however, that "it is hard (but not impossible) to imagine that General Motors or the AMA or the SEC can be endowed with such political significance that their reformation can be made the source of a popular upheaval and that, in the process, all other differences will be set aside").[11]

Much of its future, of course, hinges on the use its enemies choose to make of the considerable counterpower they collectively possess, for populism certainly antagonizes an impressive range of have-much types:

Clearly, stockholders would have less money from their holdings.

The top 5 to 20% income earners and wealth holders would find their tax bills sharply increased; and summer homes and European vacations would be more difficult to achieve.

Some respected citizens would be indicted and convicted of criminal offenses—the kind that don't show up on police blotters, but that do take money out of the pockets of millions of us, and that do threaten the health and lives of many of us.

General Motors wouldn't be nearly as big and powerful as it is today, the Rockefeller Foundation would have less money to do "good works" with, since its taxes would be higher.

If Harvard or Columbia wanted to expand its facilities at the expense of a Black or Italian or Jewish neighboring community, that neighborhood would have the clear legal right—and the legal and professional talent— to fight that expansion; so students and professors might have to use outmoded equipment and crowded spaces.

Craft unions wouldn't be allowed to keep out Blacks or hold down the labor supply, and they might feel their economic security jeopardized.

Congressmen would be under far closer scrutiny than they are now; and business and professional people would be eating a lot fewer expense account meals.[12]

With all of this, the authors nevertheless believe that many of us will accept an end to our special favor or fix if we come to really believe that "the fix" is ending for the other guy.

Perhaps. And then again, perhaps not, though this is clearly a slender thread to hang political fortunes on in a hard-boiled society of advantage-seeking cynics like so many of us.

In any case, whether the New Populism does or does not "catch on," it is likely to continue to have four major kinds of impact on social class relationships:

Revolution will be further discouraged by the populist preoccupation with amelioristic ballot-box gains, however relatively extreme the demands appear.

Class consciousness will be intensified, and *Class antagonisms* exacerbated, by a conscious and deliberate positing of economic position as central in all else.

Class alliances inside the broad camps of haves and have-nots will be encouraged, this being especially strategic in challenging the race separatism that otherwise undermines social-class collaboration.

As it is far too early to identify the ultimate impact of this young (two-hundred-year-old) variation on radical thought, it may have to suffice to conclude that antiplutocrat populism presently remains *the* politics of class in America. And it could yet prove *the* politics of choice should our postindustrial scenario in the 1970's continue to neglect the "little man's" demand for fairness and justice, as well as his seething indignation over allegedly raw abuses of economic privilege. Construed explicitly as a movement, and not as a faction yoked to one political party or to one charismatic personality, the New Populism should continue to challenge and help to change American culture, class, and capitalism for stormy decades to come. Somebody, after all, *must* continue to ask—who owns America, and by what right?

Appendix: Senator George McGovern's Populist Anti-Inequality Proposals

Here are the highlights of Senator George McGovern's 1972 campaign economic proposals:

Personal income tax. Set top rate at 48% with other reforms. No increase on wage and salary income.* Cost: $1.4 billion a year.

Capital gains. Tax fully as ordinary income. Tax capital gains at death.* Raise: $12 billion.

Municipal bonds. Offer Federal subsidy of 50% of the interest cost to localities issuing taxable bonds. Cost: $300 million.

Mineral preferences. Abolish depletion allowances and capitalize intangible drilling expenses. Raise: $2.2 billion.

Depreciation allowances. Repeal ADR and revise industry guidelines to correspond with average lifetime of assets.* Raise: $4.2 billion.

Investment credit. Use countercyclically, if possible, only for investment increases that would not otherwise have been made.* Raise: $2.5 billion.

Tax shelters. End farm-loss, real-estate shelters. Raise: $1.2 billion.

Foreign earnings. Repeal DISC and other special treatment for income earned abroad.† Raise: $1.3 billion.

Death and gift taxes. Replace by an "accessions tax" on all recipients of sizable sums, except spouses.† Raise: no immediate revenue.

Property tax relief. Extend federal assistance to cover one-third of costs of local school systems.† Cost: $15 billion.

Employment. Provide public-service jobs to heads of households who would otherwise have to go on welfare.† Cost: $6 billion.

Social Security. Expand to cover 3 million more aged, blind, and disabled who would otherwise be on welfare, and raise minimum monthly benefits to $150.

Welfare. Provide annual minimum of about $4,000 to a family of four with no other income and unable to work. Cost: $5 billion.

* Substantially the Miami Convention position
† Substantially the primary position

Source: Business Week, September 2, 1972. P. 14.

---

1. C. Lasch, "Populism, Socialism & McGovernism," *The New York Review of Books* (July 20, 1972), p. 20.

2. Jack Newfeld and Jeff Greenfield, *A Populist Manifesto: The Making of a New Majority* (New York: Paperback Library, 1972), p. 9.

3. Jack Newfeld, "A Populist Manifesto," *New York* (July 19, 1971), p. 42.

4. Jeff Greenfield and Jack Newfeld, "Vox Populists," *New York* (April 17, 1972), p. 6.

5. Peter Barnes, "Rejuvenating an Old Cause," *New Republic* (April 29, 1972), p. 32.

6. James Q. Wilson, "Reply," *New York* (April 17, 1972), p. 9.

7. Newfeld and Greenfield, *op. cit.*, p. 22.

8. I draw here on Christopher Lasch, "Populism, Socialism and McGovernism," *The New York Review, op. cit.*

9. Newfeld and Greenfield, *op. cit.*, p. 17.

10. *Ibid.*, p. 220.

11. James Q. Wilson, "The Mucking of a New Majority," *New York* (April 3, 1972), p. 53.

12. Newfeld and Greenfield, *op. cit.*, p. 221.

5
America's Democratic Socialist Movement

Arthur B. Shostak

> "... it is just possible that the 'success' of American capitalism will accomplish what its sweatshops failed to do: make socialism politically relevant."
>
> Michael Harrington, 1970

> "... democratic socialism, not sure of all the answers, not promising sudden utopias, is the world's best hope. . . ."
>
> Norman Thomas, 1963

To better understand the part that the democratic socialist movement may play in the campaign against social inequality is to explore nearly one hundred and fifty years' worth of explicit wrestling with such questions as

the ability of a movement to adapt to changing circumstance without losing the way;
the gains and costs in collaboration with liberals and other kindred spirits of accommodationist resolve;
the evolutionary drift of the American proletariat;
the evolutionary direction of the American Labor movement;
the prospects in this country for a socialist succession to power; and
the insights of critics, friendly and otherwise.

Audacious and ambitious far beyond the talents of this writer, the agenda above nevertheless constitutes the organization of this chapter. Above all, the chapter makes plain just what kind of "homework" *you* inherit if you would claim a well-considered judgment of *the* prospects of the major alternative to capitalism in our time. Social inequality in America knows no challenger as intense and as jugular as this one—a revealing contention central to the prospects of us all in the 1970's.

I. ALLIANCE, ANYONE?

Any assessment of the democratic socialist movement in this nation at this time must begin with the impolite and gutsy question—why bother? Why not simply invest our energies in the reform of what we already have, instead of in DSM advocacy of that which may never be?

Because, as Michael Harrington, chairman of the Socialist Party, so energetically insists, democratic socialists, following Marx's lead, object to capitalism on moral, and not merely on utilitarian grounds. It is not simply that capitalism cannot work: it should not be allowed to work! Accordingly, conventional liberal reforms of our inherently decadent welfare state will simply not do! Our industrial state, based on a capitalist economy and its derivative social structure, is constitutionally unable to deal with three central problems. Specifically—

the class structure of capitalist society vitiates, or subverts, almost every effort toward social justice;

private corporate power cannot tolerate the comprehensive and democratic planning we desperately need; and

the capitalist system has an inherent tendency to make affluence self-destructive, e.g., the fundamental tendencies of late capitalist economies toward bigness and concentration has it produce goods whose social costs often exceed their social benefits.

Left to itself, Harrington concludes, "neo-capitalism, for all of its sophistication, cannot make desperately needed social investments, plan comprehensively and massively, or cope with either poverty or affluence. Socialism can." [1]

Critical in assessing the prospects of socialism in America is our understanding that the condemnation above does *not* argue in turn that our welfare state can be dismissed outright as a fraud, as a sellout deception that prevents the masses from coming to truly radical conclusions. On the contrary. If millions of us ever do endorse socialism we will probably do so because our efforts to reform our welfare state have demonstrated that we *must* go far beyond it.

This realistic perspective is what makes possible a strategic alliance between American socialists and liberals. Harrington urges his fellows to prominently fight to defend and extend the contemporary welfare state. At the same time, they are also to criticize its inherent inability to really solve fundamental social problems, and propose persuasive alternatives to it. Liberals, in turn, are urged to remain open to the discovery that their political and humanistic goals can *only* be completely achieved on the basis of a democratic socialist program. They may be cheered by emergency gains, as with tough (if temporary) Phase II Wage and Price controls. But, such short-lived adaptations are invariably reversed when brief periods of crisis innovation are followed by long-term restoration periods, by a costly return to capitalist normality. Instead of always settling for such episodic "victories" within a basically antisocial environment, liberals are expected to soon come to their senses and finally join their (patient) socialist colleagues in an overdue effort to create a radically new environment.

II. REFORM AGENDA

More specifically, advocacy of the DSM platform entails support for five far-reaching redistribution reforms, or, a case for spending more, planning more, owning more, taxing more, and permitting more. A case, in short, for earning a new constituency, caring for it, providing it with necessities, paying the considerable bills on the entire affair, and helping to make it all worthwhile. If carried off to anywhere near perfection the reform agenda would turn the social inequality situation inside out and upside down . . . a dizzying state of affairs appropriate to a concomitant and exhilarating transition to a socialist utopia.

1. APPROPRIATIONS

First among the DSM proposals for undermining the causes of social inequality is a call for government commitment to enormous dollar investments in welfare projects. Private capital, lacking substantial profit-making prospects, is unlikely to invest in slum housing, rural redevelopment, hard-core job training, and the low-return like. Therefore, society must shift resources away from the privately profitable sector of the economy into the socially necessary. A progressive income tax nationally administered appears the only source of funds equal to the gigantic appropriations at issue here.

How much should be spent, and where should it go? For openers, the socialist platform calls for immediate rescinding of the proposed 1973–74 Administration cuts in national social programs:

TABLE I. 1974 BUDGET CUTBACKS

Welfare	—reduced $1.5 billion
Medicare & Housing	—reduced $1.5 billion
Health, Education and Poverty Programs	—reduced $1.0 billion
Pensions and Retirement	—reduced $1.0 billion

Source: Herbert Rowen, "1973 Issue: Nixon's Cuts in Social Programs," *The Washington Post*, February 4, 1973, p. K–2.

Relevant here is a letter addressed to the President by twenty-three public-interest advocates and groups protesting these cuts: ". . . we would urge that before you stop programs for the many, you at least should scrutinize programs for the few. Before there are fewer libraries and hospitals and low-income apartments and sewage control systems, there should be fewer subsidized ships, less expensive drug and arms procurement, and more taxes paid by coddled corporations." [2]

After winning this goal the DSM program calls for additional funding emphasis on Federal job-creation programs. Still considered the most powerful of antipoverty programs, a guarantee of a decent job is a major DSM concern. It follows that unless we are callous enough to accept the presence of a permanent underclass of unemployed people of color and Southern Whites, we must initiate a vastly expanded, long-range program of public service employment.

Not just any program will do, only one that progressively embodies provision for personal career advancement, optional integration into civil-service career lines, and mechanisms for substantial community control. DSM advocates also expect two additional and major gains: Enlarged public employment should help us improve our shoddy public services, including inadequate schooling, rickety public transportation, and a general decline in public amenities; it should also promote a radical change in the organization of labor markets. It is only the fear of unemployment and income loss that has men tolerate dulling industrial routines, and once public policy (job guarantees) serves to dissipate this fear, industry will finally be compelled to design work that honors the worker and helps us enhance our lives on and after work hours.

2. PLANNING

Clearly, more than investment must be socialized. Hence, a second proposed reform has government move four-square into social planning. Many leading conservatives are sophisticated enough today to understand that the "chaotic" growth of modern society is no longer tolerable, and planning has therefore become the most characteristic expression of the new capitalism.

Socialists, sensitive to the far-reaching hazards entailed in manipulative and privilege-promoting planning, press three subreforms:

planning must include adequate, and not just token funding for social programs;

planning must be comprehensive; it must include long-range projections and a conscious coordination of government policies; and

planning must be democratic; the people, rather than corporations with government subsidies, should decide priorities.

The subgoals, or planning that is massive, comprehensive, and democratic, are in turn all bent to a special socialist concern with the arcane art of attempting to "manage" the future.

Specifically, it is proposed that there be an Office of the Future in the White House. Each year, in Harrington's blueprint, the President will offer a Report on the Future—complete with projections ranging five, ten, or even twenty years ahead. This will be submitted to a Joint Congressional Committee where it will be debated, amended, and then presented to the entire Congress for decision. Such a process could help us finally establish the broad priorities of our society, and annually monitor the result of past efforts.

3. NATIONALIZATION

A third proposed reform has government gradually take over the ownership of private corporations. What is proposed is not a sudden, wholesale take-over by the state, but a steady, long-term process progressively abolishing private decisions in favor of democratic direction of enterprise. It is argued here, for example,

> that the right to locate, or relocate a plant in a given area can no longer be conceded to be a private matter; for in order to engage in regional planning the geography of employment has to be publicly determined; and
>
> that the right to set profit goals can no longer be conceded to be a private matter, for government cannot trust to the good conscience of the corporation.

What is proposed is a gradual "buying into" corporate control—on behalf of the government (the people)—sometimes literally, and sometimes figuratively.

American socialists are sensitive, of course, to the question of "why bother?"—as the socialist parties of Western Europe have recently abandoned their once-sacrosanct insistence upon social ownership, and now dismiss the classic case for nationalization as irrelevant. Instead, they put their trust in rational, plan-oriented professional managers who have recently taken over from anachronistic "robberbaron" capitalists. These new-styled executives are judged smart enough to identify their best interests with observing the broad priorities of the Socialist State. At the same time the government is expected to claim prerogatives sufficient to promoting the kind of full-employment policies that yield a growing fund for social spending.

This projected "honeymoon" of calculating private enterprise managers and a bountiful and tolerant socialist government leaves Harrington and others unconvinced. They distrust the European socialist notion of the state programming a market economy with social goals—and cite two particular notions in explanation of their preference for the older model of public control over management:

> First . . . the recent experience of the Continental social democrats confirms the tendency of the corporations to try to dominate, rather than obey, the government that is supposed to be controlling them.
>
> And second, it is now possible to have a relatively painless transition to social ownership. . . .[3]

This last point, or our new-found ability to nationalize in a very practical, unapocalyptic way, cannot be overestimated in explanation of our native persistence in nationalization advocacy.

How? Just how might it be achieved—relatively painlessly? The mechanics of this third reform are intriguing. Structural changes under consideration include

> abolishing the voting rights of all speculative, short-term shareholders; this would make it clear that many of the transactions on the stock market are nothing but a socially approved form of gambling—and an enormous waste of resources and energy in a parasitic operation without real economic function;
>
> instituting the right of the government to act as if it were the majority stockholder in all major industries, but without taking legal title; when private egotism leads to antisocial behavior, the government would see to a change;
>
> adopting a confiscatory tax on the stock holdings of the rich, as through prohibitions on large inheritances;
>
> establishing a government investment bank as the recipient of the stock paid as a death duty, and also of the savings of the workers; and
>
> controlling profits through selective price and wage controls in an inflationary period; requiring big companies to open up their books and justify any increase in process before an independent board; and using a vigorous tax policy.

None of these changes means enough alone. They only come into their own as interrelated part of a gradually unfolding, and thereby politically tenable, comprehensive policy aimed at steadily reducing the rights of private property in the means of production.

4. TAX REFORM: ALLIANCE AID

The three structural reforms reviewed thus far—

> expansion in government spending on social needs;
> expansion in governmental social planning and control; and
> expansion in government control over private corporations, as a preliminary to government ownership—

are matched in contentiousness and public skepticism by a fourth preoccupation of democratic socialists.

The reform in this case would have us promote a more egalitarian society through a creative and vigorous use of our tax policies. For example, "income," as presently defined by the Internal Revenue

Service is not income at all: it excludes a good portion of capital gains worth seven billion dollars a year. It does not tax the rent a middle-class family saves by owning a house, an item worth eight billion dollars a year. It exempts various state and local bonds, and so on. Harrington calmly points out that "the simple equitable act of making income equal income for purposes of tax computation would be a major contribution to social justice." [4]

Effective inheritance taxes are also cited as another important source of social funds, and an opportunity for working toward greater equality. In our nation these taxes are quite low, or quite avoidable, which amounts to the same thing. Harrington's proposal here is not likely to endear him to the "remember-me-in-your-will" set:

> In classic capitalist theory, a man must be able to leave his fortune to his children if he is to have an incentive to work hard all his life. That motive could easily be protected by providing for relatively low death duties on the *first* transfer of wealth, from father to son. This would encourage the father, while very high rates on the second transfer, from son to grandson, would give both of them a reason to strive hard.[5]

As if to ease the hazard here to fortune-hopefuls a droll Harrington sagely adds that his reform follows the "ingenious Saint-Simonian scheme of abolishing inheritance over three generations and counting on the greed of the first generation to make it indifferent to what happens to its grandchildren." [6]

Economist Robert Lekachman notes elsewhere in this connection that "in the long run, the most essential feature of the redistributionist strategy is limitation of inheritance. Just because the older John D. Rockefeller was the most efficient (and pious) buccaneer of his age, why should various Rockefellers be actual or potential governors and the unelected urban planners of metropolitan New York? For how long are plutocracy and political democracy compatible?" [7]

Equally controversial is the advocacy by some DSM members of the Negative Income Tax, one among several attractive redistribution plans that promise a guaranteed annual income. In the writings of James Tobin and other liberal economists the Negative Income Tax promises substantial socialist gains. Individuals and families above as well as below the poverty line will benefit—the working poor, as well as the unemployed, but also a segment of lower-middle-income America. The destitute will receive cash grants, while the working poor will receive benefits from income supplements. Better-off Americans, in turn, will enjoy tax remissions (the McGovern plan for minimum-income grants, a NIT variation, would have granted families between four thousand and twelve thousand dollars, either cash supplements or tax remissions worth twenty-nine billion dollars).

Exactly how redistributionist this particular DSM alternative is depends on where the cut-off point is located, the size of individual benefits, and the manner in which new revenue to finance the scheme is extracted from those above the cut-off point. Lekachman insists that "it is *possible* to transfer $43 billion from the affluent to the vast majority of Americans who earn less than $12,000 annually. It is highly *desirable* to finance the transfer by slightly higher taxes on $12,000–$20,000 incomes, and sharply increased imposts on income above $50,000." [8]

Finally, the DSM tax strategy takes special aim at the tax advantages enjoyed by stock-market investors. Harrington has very little use for such types ("parasites and gamblers") whose main form of activity on the market is legalized gambling of a sort that provides no new venture capital whatever. His point, he carefully explains, is not to penalize hard work or actual risk taking. Rather, he urges us to limit sincerely, and eventually to eliminate, the tribute society pays to passive wealth and stock gamblers:

For as the process of accumulation becomes much more social, with industry generating its own investment funds or getting them from institutions, it is absurd to pay generations of functionless coupon clippers on the grounds that their ancestors made a contribution to the economy.[9]

This is property income, Harrington intones, and it must become the target of prohibitive taxation, for it is a kind of corrosive income easy enough to distinguish from a reasonable reward for genuine present-day achievement.

Overall, then, the DSM tax plan calls for a vigorous attack on the tax labyrinth that presently favors only those who can afford clever lawyers and wily accountants. Reforms might include

imposition of an effective minimum tax on total income;
treatment of capital gains as ordinary income;
taxation of inheritances larger than $500,000 at 77 per cent rates;
phasing out of mineral depletion allowances;
repeal of the investment tax credit; and
closure of expense-allowance loopholes.

In this way the very organization of inequality itself can be undermined. And, in this way DSM partisans expect to make substantial gains in the competition for public support. Harrington contends that of all the socialist reforms current, "the use of taxes to increase justice and equality should be the most politically promising. For it would be a policy attacking the wealth of a parasite minority, and once all the out-moded rationales for favoring the rich were shattered, a majority of the people might be educated to see the value of a radical system of taxation." [10]

5. PARTICIPATORY DEMOCRACY

The last, though possibly *most* significant of the DSM challenges to social inequality, calls for socialism-from-below. At once a technique and a philosophy of action, this argument for participatory democracy advocates experimental alterations in the entire range of authority-dependency relationships—everything from management-worker to bureaucrat-client, to teacher-student, and even parent-adolescent.

Considered by sociologist Martin Oppenheimer "the essence of socialism," PD is defined by him in terms of two complementary notions:

First, that people are inherently capable of understanding their problems and expressing themselves about these problems and their solutions if given a social context in which freedom of expression is possible, that is, a situation in which one is free of personal and political hangups.

Second, that real solution to problems require the fullest participation of the people in these solutions, with the development of freedom from dependency on authorities and experts.[11]

The assumption, in short, is that the good society is one in which people will want to try to function to their fullest potential. And, conversely, a society cannot be good unless this happens.

Apropos the issue of social inequality PD has a direct and significant relevance. For example, it teaches that real education (as distinct from learning information only) cannot take place for anyone unless a situation is created in which the student is able to evaluate what goes on around him critically, without being hung up on the judgments and values of superordinates. Similarly, it lends a distinct note to DSM organizational efforts. PD involves such techniques as running meetings without agendas or presiding officers (or, at worse, rotating presiding officers);

allowing officers minimal decision-making powers away from the general meeting;

running meetings by consensus or "sense-of-meeting" decision-making;

refusing to limit discussion or debate;

letting as many executive-administrative decisions flow from the whole body as possible, without delegation of responsibilities to agents or committees; and

encouraging the body to act immediately on decisions taken, that is, dropping the artificial division between meeting and non-meeting so that in the extreme the meeting is a community and the community a virtually constant meeting.[12]

PD, in this eclectic and hazardous way, tries to approach direct democracy as nearly as possible—a critical step for a democratic socialist movement sensitive to the notion that the end is profoundly implied in the means.

A special and fascinating case of this general matter of particular democracy is that involving the call for greater involvement by workers in the traditional prerogatives of management. Stimulated by a growing labor-force anxiety over job displacement, reclassification, schedules, pacing, discipline, and the dehumanizing-like, the PD agenda here calls for the right to work-related information, the right to veto certain management moves, and a strengthened right to strike.

To be sure, the subject remains largely theoretical at present, in deference to the wavering hold of job-conscious, antisocialist trade unionism. But DSM supporters are tireless in advocating workers' control, nevertheless, and in spelling out particulars which strike directly at social inequality:

1. Workers should have the right to create their own plant safety committee, with the power to inspect, and to order any safety reforms whatsoever.
2. Workers should have full access to all job evaluation and time-motion study reports; this includes the right to veto any evaluation report and to refuse to abide by its conclusions if significant errors, inconsistencies, or prejudices in the evaluation can be shown.
3. Workers should have the veto right to oversee all hiring, transfer, promotion-demotion, recall and work assignments.
4. Workers should have the veto right to oversee all setups of production lines and the determination of production line rates.

5. Workers should have the right to elect or veto the appointment of all foremen.
6. Workers should have the right to determine all issues relating to discipline by a two-thirds majority vote of all workers in the particular work unit.
7. Workers should have access to all reports determinative of work schedules, shifts, vacations, overtime, inventory shutdowns, and so forth; along with the right to veto the implementation of any management decision relating to such.
8. Workers, by a two-thirds majority decision, should have the right to strike to insure the prompt resolution of grievances by management, including the right to resort to sitdown strikes.
9. Workers should have the right to review and to veto, if necessary, all decisions relating to plant shutdowns, relocations, layoffs, and so forth.
10. Workers should have the right, eventually, to veto decisions concerned with prices and investment.[13]

DSM advocates realistically see success here as plainly a long-term, two-stage process, the first focused narrowly on restraining and limiting management. Only years or decades thereafter, in a period of economic collapse, when management's right to make decisions unilaterally has been seriously questioned, should workers attempt to assume authority to make decisions directly.

Participatory democracy, possibly the very essence of socialism, is crystallized here in all of its promise and problematic peculiarities —in this slow-borning, but ever-stirring call for self-determination and a bill of rights for the workingman at his place of work. Few other political-reform notions challenge social inequality as keenly as does this one.

III. THE AGENT OF THE REVOLUTION

To help implement the foregoing a strategic part is written by DSM theorists for the proletariat class of every industrial nation. Accordingly, much hinges on the fundamental identification or nature of the American manual worker. Is he really a proletarian, or only a pin-up for the bourgeoisie? A peon or a dime-store prince? A worker or a Main Street hustler? The puzzle here may finally contain the key to the ultimate fate of the democratic socialistic cause in a capitalistic order.

As far as Harrington is concerned no force but labor can be true heir to the socialist vision. He welcomes the new resentment of the hard-hat as a proletariat note sounded in the very midst of capitalist America, an index of a "mood of rising enjoyments and declining satisfactions." And he comes down heavily on the cliché that a relatively high standard of living has made the American worker conservative. On the contrary, Harrington argues, "the egalitarian ideology and the lack of clearly defined limits to social mobility make for greater individual discontent among the workers."

At issue here is the popular contention that "Archie," "Joe," and the blue-collar boys down at Kelsey's Bar have become middle class in their ambitions, allegiances, politics, and outlook. This alleged *embourgeoisefication,* if credible, would compel revisions from which modern socialist theory might not recover. Not surprisingly, Harrington finds the worker as fusty and volatile as ever.

My own academic attention to the situation of the American manual worker (twenty years of campus research, several books, etc.) has me persuaded that this stress on discontent is essentially well taken. In 1969 I concluded a long analysis of blue-collar life with the contention that "America's working class is one that fears to dare, figures small angles incompetently, and makes the least-best of its life-enhancing possibilities. . . . Their plight, however, is hardly unique, and resembles nothing so much as a national epidemic or fate: Too much at present has too many members of the working class making too little of their lives." [14]

At the same time, however, I am more impressed with the hidden costs of social-class status than with either the *embourgeoisefication* or the pro-rebellion lines of analysis. It may be far more in personal harm rather than in fantasies of stopping at the Hilton that the center of the blue-collar ethos can be located. It may be in a special kind of defeat, one that Marx correctly anticipated but incorrectly expected to animate its victims, that the seemingly well-off, goods-acquiring American proletariat makes his (second-rate) peace with his situation. The "dues" for remaining a member of the working class (even in the lower levels of white-collar sales and clerical posts) may be higher, and more enervating, than readily recognized.

Much is made by the Angry Worker fans of recent studies that document what we hardly need studies to find out—that many are bored to near rage with their jobs. The controversial HEW study *Work in America* goes on to explain that in the early 1970's

the accident rate is increasing, while the productivity rate is falling;
less than 25% of all blue-collar workers would choose the same job if they had a chance to choose over; and

perhaps 70% of all employed will never receive a private pension check; even though a large percentage may be employed in firms with pension plans. . . .[15]

Barren of initiative, most of the jobs involved above are "dead ends" —a realization widespread in the ranks, but not with a consequence that change-eager socialists might anticipate.

Critics of work-place exploitation seize on the HEW findings as an exciting forerunner of constructive discontent-to-come. But they do so only in ignorance of a very contrary interpretation advanced recently by sociologists Richard Sennett and Jonathan Cobb. After perhaps five hundred hours of conversation with one hundred and fifty Bostonians, the writers conclude that sacrifice is, in the condition of most blue-collarites, "the most fundamental action you can perform that proves your ability to be in control; it is the final demonstration of virtue when all else fails." [16]

In other words, the people studied are far more self-accusatory than they are revolutionary, far more indignant with themselves than with anyone or anything else. "The whole point of sacrificing for their children is that their children *will* become unlike themselves." For these are working-class (blue- and white-collar) families where the father "doesn't ask the child to take the parents' lives as a model but as a *warning*." Voices that do not speak with any confidence that they deserve better than they are getting, these workers hold out the prospect of an enormous group of Americans upon whom the wound of class is transferred from generation to generation.

Incipient revolutionaries? Hardly. And not because of self-inflating ways. Not as long as self-flagellation remains vital for a sense of proletarian well-being.

As if to compound the inauspicious nature of it all, an otherwise admiring reader of Harrington parts with him sharply in this matter. Unpersuaded that blue-collarites, even those who escape the immobilizing effects of extreme self-defamation, are really "closet" leftists, the critic dismisses this delusionary hope with the contention that "a middle class (even though a 'lower' one) that takes up the aggrieved tone of deprivation will freeze up the very sources of social reform rather than lead to the more extensive goals of revolution." [17]

How important is any of this? Can socialism go forward without a blue-collar vanguard? Many concerned parties think not:

The historic role of industry and of the industrial proletariat, and of the ethic of co-operation, was central to the Marxian system. . . . If we can no longer believe in that historic role, then socialism, as an intellectual system, is no longer relevant to our society and our concerns. The part that the proletariat was to have played is not a piece of kindling to be thrust into any hands whatever.[18]

If the American proletariat, then, is far more resigned than it is rebellious, the implications may be profound indeed.

IV. THE PROMISED LAND: SLOUCHING TOWARD A NEW JERUSALEM

In the comparably heady matter of a socialist utopia, theorists since Marx have generally followed his lead in refusing to offer a blueprint for postcapitalist society. Occasional attempts at describing "Socialist Man" have usually conceded much to the Marxian contention that he will have to define himself in a process of self-creation that really cannot be known in advance. In the course of the last fifty years, however, conflict-ridden attention in the real world has begun to replace theoretical neglect. Today, both inside and outside of countries where Marxists hold power, discussion of socialist theory is not complete without bold reflection on the impending new birth of socialist *Gemeinschaft*.[19]

Harrington's neo-Marxian starting point in *Socialism* is the twin demand made upon man by both the realistic and the visionary tasks. Utopias are imminently practical, he insists, for without a vision the practical day-to-day efforts of crisis-oriented men are not likely to remain directed to a unified goal. Yet, paradoxically, the utopia that guides the DSM must be recognized as far distant in order to retain its immediate potency. Pretending that the utopia has been realized, or, that it can be achieved by one last desperate (and ruthless) push, has been the Achilles heel of modern socialism since 1917. Harrington sees this false utopianism as a tragic rationalization for tyranny, and castigates despotic states that call themselves "socialist" as betrayers of the dream.

Recommended instead is sensitive accommodation to a two-stage model of transition to utopian socialism. In the first stage all effort is bent to improving the lot of the have-nots living under capitalism. As this process contains the seeds of its own undoing (fatal internal contradictions inherent in capitalism, etc.) the nation can be expected to move naturally and inevitably toward democratic socialism. Only at such a time, however, when men have learned to live cooperatively through a long common and constructive experience of mutual struggle, and, when postscarcity abundance is a common and incontrovertible economic fact, can the second, or total socialist stage be fully achieved.

And what of this ultimate stage, this age-old dream state of modern socialism? Harrington takes a hard-nosed approach to what often in less capable hands has proved a mushy, unconvincing mélange. Socialists, he soberly reminds us, "do not foresee an ultimate stage of human existence in which all questions are answered and all conflicts resolved. Even in the very best of societies the democratic majority must be on the alert." [20] As with the tenets of the New Populism, and keenly distinct from a good deal of counterculture analyses, utopian possibilities are relegated to generations as yet unborn for specification of particulars—and possibilities.

In seeming odds with the Harrington orientation, and almost alone among modern socialist theorists, the European emigré and philosopher Herbert Marcuse has recently tried to "speak the unspeakable" and outline the contours of the society beyond repressive domination. Believing *the* failure of socialism to date to have been a failure of imagination, Marcuse unabashedly seeks to reintroduce a utopian cast to socialist theory. A complex and pessimistic man, he is committed to the bleak notion that one-dimensional (capitalistic) society undermines *all* progress (via the "catastrophe of liberation"), skillfully hiding evidence at the time of its own creeping totalitarianism. Nevertheless, his special contribution comes in exploring the utopian vision of the end of all psychic repression and the transformation of man's instinctual structures.

Elements of his eclectic work are immediately brow-arching, and commonly leave him at odds with socialist colleagues:

Unlike the optimistic Marx, Marcuse contends that growing well-being does not create an appetite for socialism.
Unlike the reckless Reich, Marcuse avoids advocating simple sexual freedom as the answer to social repression.
Unlike the wishful Harrington, Marcuse sees little evidence of a new proletariat or the stirrings of new prosocialist forces in the labor force.

His utopian expectations are no less controversial:

The achievement of a rational society is likely to end the need for art. For art is only a promise of unfulfilled happiness.

The achievement of a rational society is likely to end the need for politics. For the socialist utopia will include a grand synthesis of political differences.

The achievement of a rational society is likely to end all advertising and indoctrinating media of information and entertainment.

The achievement of a rational society is likely to end the liberty to "break the peace wherever there still is peace and silence, to be ugly and to uglify things, to ooze familiarity, and to offend against good form. . . ."

Overall, Marcuse seeks a new sensibility which will unify art and technology in a "society in which the abolition of poverty and toil terminates in a universe where the sensuous, the playful, the calm, and the beautiful become forms of existence and thereby the *form* of the society itself."

Leaving particulars aside, the foregoing helps to make a larger point altogether: Whatever one makes of the blueprint, it is plain that Marcuses's celebrity status has helped alter DSM theory for some time to come. Utopian particulars, Harrington (and Marx) to the contrary, *are* now agenda items—and the DSM appeal is probably all the greater for that.

Utopianism of Marcuse's persuasion, however, does raise one additional and disturbing point of consequence. Harrington's disinclination to dare the kind of social forecasting that Marcuse thinks strategic points to another divisive controversy inside the DSM. For many socialists are reluctant to embrace the elitism they think is inherent in Marcusian analysis. They are dissuaded from concluding, with the Marcusians that they have been granted a perception of reality that is exempt from the prismatic distortions under which others suffer.

Given its assumptions, Marcuse's logic is both consistent and plausible:

1. "In the last analysis, the question of what are true and false needs must be answered by the individuals themselves."
2. "But only in the last analysis: that is, if and when they are free to have their answer."
3. "As long as they are indoctrinated and manipulated, their answer will not be their own."

While this bespeaks an initial belief then, in egalitarianism, it finally permits a rejection of majority sentiment on the ground that popular opinion has been corrupted by a circumscribing mode of life. While the oppressed and the downtrodden may have the capabilities for developing into individuals of talent and quality, capitalist society has so exploited their weaknesses as to reduce them to one-dimensional caricatures of their potential selves.

Marcuse will and does presume to speak for these victims. This, in turn, leads a critic to castigate him as a "deeply conservative man, committed to reason as the only corrective and willing to follow that reason wherever it may lead."

Are people indoctrinated?—then we must censor all thought and words which might mislead them. Are people ignorant of their own needs?—then we will, for a time, have a dictatorship of the educated elite. Is human nature too frail for freedom?—then we must create a new man.

It is all very logical, the critic concedes. "But you cannot organize the sea." [21]

Others, of course, see it differently. As political scientist Andrew Hacker explains, a Marcusian may feel himself ennobled in being exempted from deferring to popular "opinion" as it is currently shaped:

[The theory] confirms his belief that he alone knows the true needs of the underclasses, that to him has been given the task of defining political goals for those who are unable to perceive their own historic interests.[22]

Who then can discern the shape and particulars of a utopia worth living and dying for? Marcuse nominates the Radical-Intellectual in the here and now; Harrington, the New Man who will be created at some distant time when a peaceful transformation to socialism will be far behind us. Marcuse slips into the Orwellian notion that all are equal, but some are (presently) *more* equal than others; Harrington prefers to urge patience until all are more nearly equal—in truth. Once again, the sharp difference in interpretation and values helps make plain the enormous toll this fascinating topic (the End that the Means were always supposed to be all about) has always extracted from the socialist movement.

V. SOCIAL INEQUALITY

Pulling all the foregoing together, then, is it likely that the democratic socialist movement will have much of an impact on social inequality in America in the foreseeable future?

For one thing, the five reform proposals of the modern democratic socialist movement promise extraordinary *redistribution*—in the first case, of government support, and thereafter of planning and government ownership, tax targets, and self-governance. The radical reform call here is to distribute *power* as well as income . . . substantially away from the haves and to the have-nots. Full-employment fiscal and monetary policy, buttressed by guaranteed public jobs, nationalized industries, and Federal social planning, should rapidly restructure labor markets and help us enhance our own job satisfactions. Similarly, effective taxation of inheritances, stock gains, and the unearned like can, in a generation, dramatically limit the seamy power of money over our law-making and political processes.

It may be argued that we have attempted much of this already, to no special avail. To which contention DSM enthusiasts heatedly reply—Not so, not even nearly so!

The failures of Great Society policies were failures of custodial liberalism, not of radical policies. Great Society liberalism was a well-intentioned prescription for the better preparation of poor people for the same old capitalist rat race. Social democrats require, as Lyndon Johnson did not, structural change in the ownership of resources and the location of power.[23]

Redistribution strategies, DSM followers conclude, have not failed. Rather, even as Chesterton explained of Christianity, they have scarcely been tried.

To more fully appreciate the potential DSM impact on social inequality, however, is to go beyond these five transitional matters to two additional reform objectives which, albeit far more distant yet, nevertheless animate the entire DSM phenomenon in our time. Specifically, there is a cardinal socialist ultimatum that calls for the end of compulsory labor, and another that calls for the abolition of money. To consider both ideals is to remain relevant to the present as they have "some bearing on tomorrow's urgent trade union negotiations and on the next welfare measure in the legislature. It was, for example, a prophetic notion of more dignity for human beings which led the British socialists in 1945 to reject a means test for the new social services they were providing."[24]

Apropos the abolition of work and money in a new and revolutionary order, the DSM scenario expects much from automation, cybernation, and leisure. To be sure, in the immediate future there is so much work that needs to be done that the next several generations will probably labor much as we do. But, in a cybernetic era, when the basic needs of all mankind are provided for, and productivity still grows, men may be forced to live without compulsory work. Instead, in a new economy of abundance, they are expected to find within themselves and their mutual relationships, rather than in external necessity (as at present), an enlarging reason for living. Every citizen, Marx rhapsodized, is expected to become a Renaissance Man . . . this, a most auspicious foundation for unprecedented social equality. ("In a Communist society," Marx and Engels wrote, "there will be no painters, but only highly developed men who, among other things, paint.") [25]

As for the abolition of money, socialism argues that as long as access to goods and pleasures is rationed according to the possession of money, there is a pervasive venality, an invitation to miserliness and hostility to one's neighbor. Particularly in the area of necessities, Harrington insists, "no one should be required to choose between needs or to sacrifice them in order to get luxuries—and that is what money makes inevitable." [26]

Socialism therefore strives to have more and more goods and services provided free, including medicine, housing, transportation, a healthy diet, and others. It remains true, of course, that nothing is really ever free in the economist's sense of the term, and there would surely remain a collective payment for these goods. At the same time, however, the related change in moral atmosphere created by such a new mode of distribution will be profound.

Socialism, then, is *not* alone a program for redistributing power and wealth, as fundamental a goal in reducing social inequality as that is. Socialism is animated as well by a vision of a new and revolutionary order. And it asserts this through its campaign of seeking, in the distant but conceivable future, to abolish compulsory work and the rationing system of money as far as is humanly possible. In this critical and mind-boggling way socialism boldly proposes to end that invidious competition and venality which, because scarcity has allowed no other alternatives, we have timidly come to think are inseparable from humanity.

As Harrington tersely explains, "under socialism there will be no end to history—but there may be a new history." [27]

SUMMARY

Again, we turn back to the overarching question: Will the DSM soon have a substantial impact on correcting social inequalities in our country? If the deciding matter was only the existence of possibly fatal contradictions in capitalism, or an ambitious and potent agenda for change, or the mere presence of a restless potential block of change-agents (workers, radical youth, etc.), or the guiding vision of a world beyond work and money, a positive answer would emphatically recommend itself. But the issue is nowhere that clear. And the DSM cause continues to struggle uphill in our coopting, cuddling, and crippling capitalist social order to merely gain public attention, better yet earn the advocacy of significant publics.

Perhaps the most fitting closing thoughts, then, are appropriately borrowed again from DSM Chairman Michael Harrington. He is "not at all sure that there will be a socialist alternative to Communism and the welfare state. It is certainly quite possible that the twenty-first century will belong to bureaucratic collectivism and that the dream of human self-emancipation will turn out to have been mankind's noblest deception. . . ." Nevertheless, Harrington quietly insists that "after so many failures and betrayals the socialism defined here does not pretend to be the wave of the future. It is simply our only hope." [28]

APPENDIX

Just before his death in 1934, Morris Hillquit, considered by many the prime mover of the Socialist Party of America from 1901 on, penned the following:

> I am a Socialist because I cannot be anything else. I cannot accept the ugly world of capitalism, with its brutal struggles and needless suffering, its archaic and irrational economic structure, its cruel social contrasts, its moral callousness and spiritual degradation.
>
> If there were no organized Socialist movement or Socialist party, if I were alone, all alone in the whole country and the whole world, I could not help opposing capitalism and pleading for a better and saner order, pleading for Socialism.
>
> By violating my conscience, I might have made peace with the existing order of things and found a comfortable place among the beneficiaries of the system. I might have joined one of the political parties of power and plunder and perhaps attained to a position of influence and "honor." I might have devoted my life to the acquisition of wealth and possibly accumulated a large fortune. But my apparent success would have been dismal failure. I should have been deprived of all the joys of life that only an inspiring social ideal can impart, of the pleasure and comradeship of the best minds and noblest hearts in all lands, and, above all, of my own self-respect.

Having chosen and followed the unpopular course of a Socialist propagandist, I am entirely at peace with myself. I have nothing to regret, nothing to apologize for.[29]

1. Michael Harrington, *Socialism* (New York: Saturday Review Press, 1970), p. 291.
2. Herbert Rowen, "1973 Issue: Nixon's Cuts in Social Programs," *The Washington Post*, February 4, 1973, p. K-2.
3. Michael Harrington, *Socialism, op. cit.*, pp. 296–97.
4. *Ibid.*, p. 305.
5. Michael Harrington, "Why We Need Socialism in America," *Dissent* (May–June 1970), p. 270.
6. *Ibid.*
7. Robert Lekachman, "Toward a Reordered Economy," *Dissent* (Fall 1972), p. 582.
8. *Ibid.*
9. Harrington, "Why We Need Socialism in America," *Dissent, op. cit.*, p. 270.
10. *Ibid.*
11. Martin Oppenheimer, "The Limitations of Socialism: Some Sociological Observations on Participatory Democracy," in C. George Benello and Dimitrios Roussopoulous (eds.), *The Case for Participatory Democracy: Some Prospects for a Radical Society* (New York: The Viking Press, 1971), p. 282.
12. *Ibid.*, pp. 277–78.
13. Adapted from Jack Rasmus, *Workers' Control: A Reader on Labor and Social Change* (New York: Random House, 1973).
14. Arthur Shostak, *Blue-Collar Life* (New York: Random House, 1969), pp. 290–91.
15. HEW, *Work in America* (Washington, D.C.: Government Printing Office, 1973), p. 211.
16. Richard Sennett and Jonathan Cobb, *The Hidden Injuries of Class* (New York: Knopf, 1973), p. 172.
17. Garry Wills, book review of M. Harrington, *Socialism* in *The New York Times Book Review* (April 30, 1972), p. 1.
18. Eugene Kamenka, "The Old, Old Left," *New York Review of Books* (November 20, 1969), p. 42.
19. See in this connection Stanley Moore, "Utopian Themes in Marx and Mao," *Dissent* (March–April 1970), pp. 170–76.
20. Harrington, *Socialism, op. cit.*, p. 1.
21. Richard Goodwin, "The Social Theory of Herbert Marcuse: Which Side Is He On?" *Atlantic Monthly* (June 1971), p. 85.

22. Andrew Hacker, "Philosopher of the New Left," *The New York Times Book Review* (March 10, 1968), p. 34.
23. Lekachman, *op. cit.*, p. 585.
24. Harrington, "Why We Need Socialism in America," *Dissent, op. cit.*, p. 280.
25. *Ibid.*, p. 285.
26. *Ibid.*, p. 286.
27. *Ibid.*, p. 287.
28. The entire quotation in the paragraph above is from Harrington, *Socialism, op. cit.*, p. 10.
29. *Loose Leaves from a Busy Life* (New York: 1934), p. 331.

6
Ethnicity, Ethnic Power, and Social Inequality

Arthur B. Shostak

> "*The task is to discover what America is, or might yet be. No one, of course, can address that larger issue without coming to terms with his own ethnic particularity. . . . The point of becoming ethnically alert and self-possessed is not self-enclosure; it is genuine community, honest and unpretending.*"
>
> Michael Novak
> *The Rise of the Unmeltable Ethnics,*
> 1972, p. XVI.

> "*The mobilization of ethnic groups may reflect the traumas of casting off tradition, but it may also portend innovative political forms for the future, beyond modernity.*"
>
> Cynthia H. Enloe
> *Ethnic Conflict and Political Development,* 1973, p. 274.

If the political philosophies reviewed in this chaper*—conservatism, liberalism, the New Populism, and democratic socialism—are to make a substantial impact on social inequality in America, they will have to penetrate the "protective screen" created by a relatively

---

* "Ethnicity, Ethnic Power, and Social Inequality," by Arthur B. Shostak. This essay was originally titled "Ethnic Revivalism, Blue-Collarites, and Bunker's Last Stand" and appeared in *Soundings*: An Interdisciplinary Journal, LVI (Spring 1973), pp. 68–82. The entire issue of *Soundings* in which this essay was printed has been published as a Torchbook by Harper and Row under the title *The Rediscovery of Ethnicity* (1973).

new phenomenon on the American scene—the recent proliferation of White Ethnic Power.

Modeled in open admiration and envy after the Black Power Movement of the late 1960's, the fresh and frenetic revival of White Ethnic Power in the early 1970's has swept the urban and blue-collar scene. It brings in its wake the promise of exceptional gains in personal autonomy, family relationships, and community rehabilitation.

For my part, however, I have genuine doubts about the reality of this ethnic revival, the potency of ethnic blueprints, and the motives of certain revival enthusiasts. The chapter below presents a discussion of these misgivings, accompanied by an alternative and mutually exclusive interpretation of the same phenomenon dwelled upon by revival fans in support of their approach. I close with a series of prescriptions for reform, many of which are linked to the class-based New Populism and socialism of chapters 4 and 5. These prescriptions promise much more than do those of the ersatz *machismo* model of Ethnic Power.

At stake in this critical and current controversy are both our preferred definition of personal selfhood and our mutual alliance. We either can rely once again upon narrow Old Country and blood ties, or, instead, we can choose to reduce inequality by reinvigorating local neighborhood and social-class binds. What we *cannot* do is to delay considered personal resolve, yours and mine, very much longer.

Allowing for all of our crystal-ball-reading problems, it is nevertheless vital to ponder just how inequality in America might be altered by the Great Ethnic Awakening, clearly one of the most significant (and least predicted) social developments in our Age of the Mass Society. Is inequality substantially challenged, or merely trifled with? Can the ethnic revival, the post-'60's resurgence of interest in Old Country identification, upset the WASP social hegemony (and its corollary, the Horatio Alger myth of attainable individual success)? Or, will it operate instead to exacerbate long-standing tensions inside the multiethnic bloc of have-nots (poor and working class alike)? Is privilege advantaged by our newfound resort to Old World traditions for warmth and comfort otherwise increasingly rare in our harshly competitive social order? Or, is privilege keenly undermined by an expansion of social vision, one which has the have-nots thinking anew of how life might be better lived—even if only in romanticized fantasies of an Old World "Golden Past" that probably never was.

As part of our deliberate overreach in this ambitious little book I want to share some unusual speculations of mine with you in this connection. While I am inclined to make less of the Awakening than many of my more excitable colleagues I also expect a greater lasting impact on class inequality from this phenomenon than do many other social analysts. Overall, I see vital connections here to the promotion in blue-collar ranks of a "square" style of life culture —one profoundly at odds with privilege maintenance. I also see important connections to a begrudging tolerance for the hip ways of "Mike" and "Gloria"—again, at an important cost to the maintenance of the social-class status quo. In many ways I am drawn to the argument that ethnicity and religious affiliation outweigh social class as a factor in maintaining fundamental divisions in our society. But, here as elsewhere, I reject the related Parkian proclivity to say that things are working out to everyone's advantage and apparent satisfaction.

I get ahead of myself, however, and have meant only to introduce —and not to foreclose—discussion of a fascinating aspect of the inequality mosaic.

I.

There are times when I can almost hear some twentieth-century equivalent of Mr. Dooley, Finley Peter Dunne's sagacious bartender of the early 1900's, leaning forward over his highly polished bar top to softly ask in a magical Irish lilt: "My boy, privately now and only between us, how really real is this so-called Ethnic Revival? Why the big hoorah at *this* time? And why the blarney about its medicinal properties? Will grown men never tire of the outgrown playthings of their youth?" Puzzled in like fashion, and especially interested in its equality possibilities, I want to explore our joint concern below, Dooley's and mine, and push further to suggest an alternative interpretation of and prescription for the social class discontents that some students of ethnicity are now linking to the Great Ethnic Awakening—whatever that is.

II

Four years ago, in a monograph exploring the life-styles of men in the blue-collar ranks and his more numerous conservative, and older, associates, I urged that new attention be paid to the persistence of ethnicity in the life-style of all blue-collarites.[1] Now I find myself perplexed by just that development. For what I see about me in the way of attention being paid combines so much bombast, so little refinement, and so possibly misguided a prescription for life as to leave me seriously concerned lest blue-collar white ethnics take our flurry of academic interest seriously at all.

Bombast ingloriously substitutes for empirical evidence of the existence of the very ethnic revival itself. It would seem fair to expect certain kinds of hard data from revival enthusiasts (or denigrators) that go beyond the insistence "Well, everyone just knows it!"

For example, has anyone thought to investigate longitudinal changes in the number and audience of our foreign-language radio shows, newspapers, and magazines? After adjusting data here for our record-setting immigrations of recent years (373,000 in 1970 alone, the second highest number since 1924), this material on followership could be combined with that on recent changes in the dues-paying rolls of ethnic organizations to reveal much about the hard substance really inside of revival ballyhoo. Similarly, attention might profitably be paid to changes occurring over time in the intermarriage rates among our no longer insular nationalities, and across the "border" that separates hyphenated Americans from British-Americans (as Michael Novak suggests we rechristen the WASPS). Finally, research might extend beyond tried-and-true indices (such as crowd attendance at ethnic holiday parades and court records of applications for the Americanization of Old Country names) to some more venturesome and potentially revealing new components of the scene, e.g., the stress apparently no longer placed on ethnicity in parochial schools by modern lay teachers, and the lack of stress on ethnicity by parents who shop for private schooling or who favor enactment of the voucher plan for subsidized private schooling for all.

Without such data we are sorely handicapped. And unless properly collected, even snippets of data that do become available do not always carry us much further ahead. Typical is the problem posed by large-scale travel statistics that verify an impressive amount of ethnic American travel back to the Aulde Sod. Not only is the subject clouded by the recency of the détente which has made such travel tenable (as to Eastern European nations) but the data grievously fail to separate travelers by social class or age. If disproportionately few ethnics who are both under forty-five years of age and of blue-collar status are flying "home" to "see the family tree" (as a British airlines ad beckons), the travel surge might be considered more an index of desperation than of confirmation; that is to say, more a return to fading memories by sentimental and well-heeled oldsters than a proud claiming of new roots by tradition-hungry and meaning-seeking younger working-class ethnics.

Is there an ethnic revival then, or isn't there? Plainly, we just do not know. And we are not helped by the dust cloud raised here by politicians of every persuasion in lusty quest of this or that real or imagined ethnic bloc vote. This much *is* clear: ethnic-pride ensigns, leagues, rallies, and media celebrity status do not alone an ethnic revival make.

III

Equally clear, if no less perplexing, is the remarkable revival of interest in ethnicity by men of letters. Why? Two explanations stand out in this matter. First, like the Blacks before them, in the 1960's, the white ethnics have fairly well forced themselves on the consciousness (and conscience) of the intellectual community in recent years. And second, men of ideas are—many of them—looking full circle back to their personal second-generation origins (in many cases), or to their romanticized notions of ethnic origins, for new clues to living the Good Life in a sanitized Sears Roebuck/Disneyland world too blah and banal for their still robust appetites.

There is first, then, the issue of the "uncouth" clamor raised in blue-collar neighborhoods by white ethnics who are raucously demanding—everything! Not just "law and order," as the mocking and derogatory media overstress, but also tax reductions, a return to educational fundamentals, enlargement of the consumer advocacy role of government, and equity with people of color in the distribution of scarce (and inadequate) social welfare expenditures. "You all have been getting yours for long enough," the battle cry goes. "Now we want ours!"

First given clear expression in the Wallace campaign of 1968, this motif assaults the popular intellectual rendering of an Affluent (Galbraithean) and Equal Society inside of which the vast majority of "end-of-ideology" manual workers are (credit-card) happy and (Big Labor) secure. But even as it took the Triple Deaths (Kennedy, King, Kennedy) to compel a far more honest understanding of the harshness and brutishness common in life, so also has it taken the brutal murders of the Yablonskies, the savage crippling of Joe Columbo, and the "self-destruct-on-Skag" habit of blue-collar veterans of Vietnam to shake the false euphoria and complacency out of the intellectual view of blue-collar life.[2] Why the revival, then, of egghead interest in manual workers? Possibly because the piercing outcry of blue-collar discontent—and the enormous "dues" of neglect in the form of the decay and terror of the cities both egghead and worker uneasily share—has forced men of letters to take note!

A shopworn scenario, you think, one with a strong ring of familiarity? Of course, as in most important regards it stays close to the more inclusive pace-setting Black-White scenario of the last fifteen years. Save in this one critical difference: Many degreed Caucasian interpreters of white ethnicity, themselves often among the first of their own Old-Country bloc to attain intellectual distinction (by British-American standards), take now to press to publicly ruminate about the meaning of it all and most especially, about the ethnic ethos or positive social inequality they plaintively wish to somehow preserve in their own homogenizing suburbias. Mixing unequal parts of nostalgia (the "white lie" variety), recrimination (the British-Americans, again as heavies), and romance (Novak's New Ethnic Consciousness, a sublime achievement in Maslow-like universal self-actualization) the white commentators "go home" as was never possible before in their strained and once-removed commentary on black realities.

They posit new interpretations of social mobility "failure":

The Irish in New York represent a way of life that never was Irish. The Irish always were poor and they measured value by other than material things. They sang and told stories and used words for entertainment. Their descendants in New York can't wait to get into the banking business.[3]

And they posit new models of social-mobility success—even if of a strained and desperate variety: Little Italy plays host weekends to "Saturday's Italians," those prospering overweight sons of leaner immigrant fathers who drive in now from suburbia on weekends to replenish their ever-diminishing ethnic supplies.

They return, after all, not only for the bread, tiny bitter onions, bushels of snails, live eels and dried cod, but also to enjoy a weekend heritage that their education, blonde wives, and the English language have begun to deny them. . . . It is only with a trunk filled with Italian market produce that a Saturday Italian can face six days in the suburbs.[4]

Above all, however, they make plain how much anguish, confusion, and "future shock" we *share* across our social-class and ethnic (and racial) chasms—and, in this very way, ironically undermine the erstwhile point of the alleged ethnic revival they think they celebrate.

IV

For along with the bombast-in-place-of-evidence issue touched on earlier, there is the related critical matter of the costly lack of refinement, or calibration, that so taxes the entire subject. Viewed through the wire-rimmed spectacles of the visiting "made-good" ex-local boy, the problems of the blue-collarite as a white ethnic come finally to resemble far too closely the problems one can readily expect of marginal (first-generation) intellectuals themselves: The writer longs to return to an ethos that is more Archie's defeat than his deliverance, however differently it be viewed from outside.

Blue-collar women, for example, bitterly denounce their homey prototype in Edith Bunker when I ask about this popular TV heroine in my research. They especially disown her Old Country passivity, naïveté, and doltishness. Working outside their homes and ethnic neighborhoods as many do, these freewheeling women are often aggressive, sophisticated, and mentally adroit. Long accustomed, as in the case of the culturally assimilated movie wife of "Joe," to manipulating the men folk (of all ages), modern blue-collar women more often resemble (and seem to identify with) Gloria than with Edith in the Bunker household.

Similarly, young blue-collarites of both sexes find Archie a bit hard at times to recognize, as many have either long since helped direct their fathers away from the Old Country/Bunker mold—or have grudgingly moved far away from a "lost cause" of an obsolete Old Man. And it is just this notion of chronic tension, special effort, and ultimate resolution that underlies my particular perspective on what it is that *is* bothering Bunker—and what we might all help do about it.

I see Archie hurting not so much from the loss of ethnicity the writer bemoans as from a lingering attachment to it! In many costly ways he uses his Old World ethnicity as a second-rate shield against a host of new personal and intimate demands put on him by the hardest audience to deny of all, his own family members.

Preoccupied with the white ethnic's 8 AM to 5 PM problems (the assembly-line speedup, the dead-end job ladder, the threat of technological displacement, etc.), we have paid grossly inadequate attention to the related discontents of his 5 PM to 8 AM existence. Narrowly sensitive to his after-work role as citizen, voter, and ethnic, we have paid far too little attention to him in his roles as husband, lover, father, and son. Yet it is exactly here, in a "role-crunch" that dwarfs anything the script writers for the Bunkers seem equal to, that white ethnics may especially hurt—and find yesterday's ethnicity-as-remedy irrelevant.

Where once the blue-collar male was free to be a self-centered, self-gratifying Marlboro Country cowboy, he is now expected to aspire drastically otherwise. A new role set asks him to strive for frank and genial affability with most, deep-coursing personal intimacy with some, and erotic artfulness with a very select few. His family (rather than his churchmen, ethnic spokesmen, or academic interpreters!) expect, indeed demand, that they all live now as other than muffled human beings, disappointed in life and in one another. Instead, they set their faces firmly against the Old World anxieties and divisions that would tax them so, and struggle to replace dogma and taboo with the excitement of a life engagingly explored.[5]

Not all, of course, by any means, but many. And, of these, large numbers are under thirty-five years of age, and therein lies still another key point with which I will draw to a close this espousal of a substitute analysis, one that refocuses our attention on class issues, for that of the Great Ethnic Awakening.

V

None of this is meant to gloss over significant differences inside the category of blue-collar ethnics themselves. Much of the "role crunch" is escaped by those over fifty, directly experienced by those between thirty-five and fifty, stoutly resisted by those between twenty and thirty-five, and quizzically observed by those between fifteen and twenty. Inside these age brackets a further breakdown separates foreign-born (less vulnerable) from third-generation native-born (most vulnerable), immobile (less vulnerable) from upwardly mobile (more vulnerable), and immigrant church-oriented (less vulnerable) from mainstream Catholic (more vulnerable, given Protestant-like alterations in modern Catholic attitudes and practices). When fractionized in this fashion the rich diversity of the (artificially perceived) bloc is clear, and its internal dynamism is more readily grasped. This dynamism helps explain the otherwise contradictory existence, side by side, of both traditions of interest in this essay—the worker's lingering romance with Old World ethnicity and his newer flirtation with his own version of New World modernism.

To be sure, the largest number of blue-collarites at this time stay closer to the ethnic mold than to modernistic derring-do. And this is likely to remain true through the late 1980's.[6] But given the disproportionately large bloc of youngsters coming along (twelve-year-olds are the largest age bloc in our population) this situation may already be changing, with the working class having possibly generated its own (cultural) revolutionary vanguard from within!

At present, for example, many "vanguard" blue-collarites appear to be closing social-class rifts to join comparable middle-class rebels in redoing their own native church. The so-called underground Catholic church draws them with the hope that its person-centeredness, its humanism, its erotic, sensual possibilities, and, above all, its bold incorporation of psyche-expanding encounter techniques, will help them grow as their fathers cannot (dare not?). Others look to media innovations, both sexes tuning in avidly to new radio talk shows astonishing in their sex-relations candor, and to psychoanalytic explorations of real-life dilemmas ("The Family Game," etc.). Many also turn regularly to ever bolder media columnists (Dr. Reuben, Marya Mannes, Dr. Hippocrates, etc.) in the underground as well as the conventional press, and take instruction in modernity from the glossy likes of *Playboy* and *Cosmopolitan* (where their parents stick to *True* and *True Confessions*, *Argosy* and *Photoplay*, *True Detective* and *TV/Radio/Mirror*).

Many find ethnicity inimicable to a host of personal role options that seem to require freedom from musty taboos, Old Country strictures, and xenophobic prejudice. Pace-setters among these blue-collar modernists dare to countenance guiltless premarital relations, casual trial marriages, unapologetic single parenthood, readily secured abortions, considerable sexual experimentation, easy no-fault divorce, single-adult adoptions, and other deep-reading challenges to conventional morality. Some of their leisure practices—like scuba diving, and flying four-hundred-dollar radio-controlled model airplanes—extend far beyond the borders of what "our people" have always (and only) enjoyed. What is even more, a full range of public behaviors (e.g., opting for circumcision of all male infants, choosing cremation over burial, etc.) powerfully rattle the bars of the ethnic "jailhouse."

Significantly, the more astute among such pioneers decline to blame themselves alone for the "role crunch" they find themselves challenged by. Instead, they find sources of responsibility as well in the larger social order, and especially in the inequality "dues" they have always had to pay. Accordingly, unlike their staid ethnic counterparts, many of these blue-collar moderns take seriously the case being made today for nationalized health care (that would include subsidized counseling and psychiatry), nationwide day care (that would include professional parent education), a guaranteed annual wage, earlier retirement, sabbatical leave, and the tradition-shattering like. Out of anti-ethnic discontents come pro-equality politics!

As an ethnic/modern split of such proportions has substantial political and public-policy ramifications it will undoubtedly strain affinities among blue-collarites for decades to come. But the handwriting is already on the wall. And while some ethnic purists see it only as "Clockwork Orange" graffiti, other translators such as myself read a very different message into it. Wary of the eviscerating perils of naïve assimilation ("into what?," sarcastically ask ethnic spokesmen as otherwise different as Eldridge Cleaver, Michael Novak, Rabbi Kahane, and Elijah Mohammed), America's blue-collarites will probably long continue to use ethnicity in a fashion uniquely their own.

Many rely on an ethnic vote to control their labor-union locals and insure at least some direct representation in city council chambers. Many use their informal ethnic studies (traditions, culture, philosophy, etc.) as a bulwark against the psychic toll of Toffler's "future shock," even as some lean on it also for a defense against the modernity of their own young. And large numbers are presently wringing every last ounce of aid from it as they struggle with the challenge of an extraordinary "role crunch," one that superficially appears to force a choice between the Scylla of retrograve ethnicity and the Charybdis of mass culture assimilation, between second-rate inequality *and* second-rate equality.

It is exactly at this point that "graffiti" interpretations substantially depart. For the case that would encourage a blue-collar revival of interest in its (now proud) ethnic origins is bold-facedly also a naïve and oversimplifying case *against* any further (unexamined) assimilationism, any additional loss of blue-collar distinctiveness into a Sears Roebuck/Disneyland glob, an increasingly unattractive mainstream.

To their considerable credit a variety of blue-collarites, old and young alike, already seem to grasp the hazard here of a *false* choice with keen insight. For some time now opinion shapers among them have fought to impose their *own* design on the entire situation, a design which has them seek the best of *both* options, the most that can be had from *both* ethnicity and from mass culture. Blue-collarites of this persuasion distinguish the "square" from the "plastic":

> Squareness implies a strong dose of personal and cultural scruple; Plasticity is the attempt to be fashionable without paying the price. Going to church out of religious conviction, however understood (or misunderstood), may be square; going to church for social reasons is plastic. "God Bless America" and "Semper Fidelis" are square; Lester Lanin playing the Beatles is plastic. Busby Berkeley musicals are square; *The Sound of Music* is plastic. Billy Sunday was square; Billy Graham is plastic. . . .[7]

This blue-collar amalgam of Old Country ethnicity and New World modernity I have reference to is decidedly square. Indeed, it seems increasingly unique to that social class, as the rest of the culture gravitates either toward the dead-end ethnic revival of the desperate non-White minorities, or, to the gray assimilationism of the majority mainstreamers. While many politicians, sociologists, and journalists are crudely unable to distinguish the "square" from the "plastic," and mistakenly insist our choice is only between (good) ethnicity and (bad) modernity, enough blue-collarites to possibly make a profound difference see it—and live it—otherwise.

This is *not* to romanticize their life-style proclivities, however attractive their rejection of the ersatz quality of the plastic life that cheapens or deadens everything it touches. The squareness of blue-collarites has its full share of blind spots and hazards for its holders, and for us all, though these shortcomings seem to pale alongside the comparable pitfalls of the false dichotomy commonly imagined by outside commentators.

What especially attracts about blue-collar squareness, however, is its class-based origins (fed by ethnic "springs"), its class-linked integrity, and its class-grounded openness to political populism.[8]

Some flavor of what I am driving at, of what I make of the class-inspired "graffiti" on the wall, might be better conveyed here from the "vanguard" example of Mrs. Bette Lowrey, a forty-seven-year-old suburban wife of a machinist, who was identified in 1970 by the media as meeting the expert's profile of the typical voter:

But in the flesh she also turned out to be more decent than the political projections, more complex than the statistics, and more informed than Agnew and his speech-writers took her to be. "I wish," she said, "that people would do more listening. All these kids wouldn't be rioting if they didn't have good reasons. Sometimes it takes rioting and dissent to bring change." Mrs. Lowrey, as it turned out, had a twenty-one-year-old son with long hair.[9]

Blue-collar "squares" of this ilk promote their own preferred version of a desirable mainstream, one that would have irreverence long persist in America, and one that helps keep alive the hope that diverse constituencies inside and even across our social classes can still be rallied against the impersonal, the systemic, and perhaps even the "plastic." [10]

Note that the irreverence of such blue-collarites extends to their own ethnicity, and that many such men and women decline to make a (new) false idol out of the accident of their ethnic origins. Typical is the rejection experienced here by a Polish-American millionaire deeply committed to promoting the so-called ethnic revival:

... above all, they wish they were solvent. They look at a millionaire like Piszek, realize that he has already spent a quarter of a million dollars on a handsomely bound Golden Book of Knowledge about Poland and wonder why in hell he isn't throwing some of that cash their way if he has so damned much to waste. ... The Poles ... feel that they can get all the culture they need at the parish hall or at CYO folk dances. What they want is money up front. They'd gladly call Ed Piszek "super-Pole" if he could push the Puerto Ricans out of [their neighborhood], help them pay the loan companies on time, and keep the streets clean.[11]

Hardly an inspiring agenda, and exactly the sort of thing likely to get *The New York Times* down on them. But in its unabashed honesty about priorities and its indulgent disdain for plastic airs, this Polish "Middle American" squareness is its *own* justification—and a striking qualification of the premature announcement of both *embourgeoisefication* and a Great Ethnic Awakening.

What *is* awakening in certain blue-collar quarters is a new interest in old popularist issues—along with a small and novel "vanguard" concern with cultural reforms. The absence of George

Wallace from the 1972 Presidential campaign, for example, was sorely missed by many blue-collarites (and millions of others as well). For alongside his convoluted racism was an engaging populist streak as he played to people increasingly impatient with the pieties and equivocation of established mainstream rhetoric. Wallace dared to run against banks and utilities, foundations and distant planners, bosses and ivory-tower theorists. Many of his younger supporters were and could again be blue-collar workers with no special loyalty to the old Democratic Party or to the professional labor leaders who purport to represent them.

Instead, this large and volatile section of the white working class shops about now for some new locus for its loyalties—and dreams. Its untutored and incoherent populism crops up in diverse and revealing ways—in the Lordstown revolt of the young workers; the move for school control by blue-collar neighborhood residents; their failure to seriously press for an end to the so-called pornography explosion; the remarkably fast adoption by Catholics of oral contraceptives, and the openness to a fiery kind of female spokeswomen previously laughed out of ethnic politics (e.g., Baltimore's Barbara Mikulski and Boston's Louise Day Hicks).

Often vulgar and schizophrenic, sometimes contradictory and chaotic, and not infrequently compassionate, this new blue-collar culture can still stumble—and finally prove little more than an interim experience on the way to what Dwight Macdonald condemns as "the agreeable ooze of the Midcult swamp." But then again, it might not. For, distainful of both Old Country ethnicity *and* mainstream plasticity, the vast bulk of manual workers sustain a time-honored attachment to their square blue-collar ethos even as they uneasily allow breathing space to the few, exotic cultural revisionists, or young "vanguard" moderns in their midst.

Pure ethnicity of the separatist variety called for by enthusiasts of the Awakening leaves most of these self-conscious blue-collarites cold. Many suspect it is too readily turned to "plastic." They know it for its divisive peril. And they especially reject its ability to let social-class issues go into hiding. Accordingly, in its availability for turning workers against one another, reinvigorated ethnicity comes in second best to the promotion, instead, of a "square" working-class culture—and a begrudging tolerance for the modish ways of the select blue-collar young.

And this, rather than a costly redirection of blue-collar culture itself, could continue to characterize the gropings of that social class for many years to come—in a fashion instructive and enlarging for us all—provided *we* allow for the pluralism herein entailed, and relax our misguided missionary zeal for ethnic (and not class/populist) renewal.

1. Arthur B. Shostak, *Blue-collar Life* (New York: Random House, 1969).

2. Brilliant in this connection is "Betrayed American Workers," by Richard Sennett and Jonathan Cobb, in *The New York Review of Books* (October 5, 1972), pp. 31–33.

3. Jimmy Breslin, "The True Irish Export," *New York World Journal Tribune* (March 12, 1967), pp. 6–7; see also Joe Flaherty, "The Men of Local 1268, God Bless Them All, the Last of a Bad Breed," *New York* (September 12, 1972), pp. 56–58.

4. Nicholas Pileggi, "Saturday Italians," *New York World Journal Tribune* (January 15, 1967), pp. 12, 14.

5. I draw above from a longer essay of mine, "Middle-Aged Working Class Americans at Home: Changing Expectations of Manhood," *Cornell Occupational Mental Health* (Fall 1972), pp. 2–7. See also Robert Coles, *The Middle Americans* (Boston: Little, Brown, 1971).

6. An exceptionally fine essay on such solid, and stolid, blue-collarites, "tragic victims requiring more attention and social concern than they have received thus far," is available in "Working-Class Youth: Alienation without an Image," by William Simon and John H. Gagnon, in *The White Majority*, edited by Louise Kapp Howe (New York: Random House, 1970), pp. 45–60.

7. Peter Schrag, *The Decline of the WASP* (New York: Simon and Schuster, 1971), p. 193, *passim*.

8. For my strongest public exploration of this thesis, see Arthur Shostak, "Blue-Collar Prospects—Grey, White, or Green Collar?," in *IRRA Proceedings, 1972* (Madison, Wisconsin: IRRA, 1972). Cf. "New Working Class?," *New Politics* (Fall 1972), pp. 29–43.

9. Schrag, *op. cit.*, p. 186. See also Robert E. Lane and Michael Lerner, "Why Hard-Hats Hate Hairs," *Psychology Today* (November 1970), pp. 45–49.

10. Helpful in this connection is Andrew M. Greeley, "New Ethnicity and Blue Collars," *Dissent* (Winter 1972), pp. 270–77. See also Frank Riessman, "The Backward Vanguard," *Society* (November/December 1972), pp. 104–6.

11. Mike Mallowe, "What's Polish, Has Two Legs and Finally Has Gotten Its Dander Up?," *Philadelphia Magazine* (November 1972), p. 113.

III. STRATEGIES FOR THE REDUCTION OF INEQUALITY

7
Strategies to Reduce Poverty and Inequality: An Overview*

Sally Bould Van Til

Social inequality is the result of differential rewards within the market system which grants economic well-being to some but not all. Since the vast majority obtain their economic rewards through the sale of their labor or the labor of some member of the family, the labor market is the key source of inequality in the original distribution of income. Of secondary importance in determining economic well-being for most families are the markets for land (rent) and capital. In a strictly free-enterprise system the government intervenes not at all with these market processes. However, the governments of the advanced industrialized nations have seen fit to interfere with the normal operations of markets in order to build a welfare state on the basis of social rights which each citizen claims by virtue of citizenship and membership in the community.[1] Welfare-state institutions operate by and large outside the market,[2] but do have some direct effect upon the market and hence upon the degree of inequality. Originally conservatives feared, and liberals hoped, that the implementation of the welfare state would result in a radically more equal society. That prediction obviously has not been met, either in America or in Western Europe. This section will examine briefly

* The author would like to thank Howard Harlan for his suggestion that this discussion should examine strategies to end poverty.

some of the institutions of the welfare state and its strategies to reduce inequality and poverty.

The welfare state is a collection of institutions outside of the market which seeks to protect citizens from some of the ravages of the unequal free-enterprise distribution of resources. As such, it represents a modification of the free-market principles upon which modern capitalist economic structures were built. Welfare-state institutions tend to take one of two forms. The first is a universal form resulting in primary institutions which serve all or nearly all of the population. One important example of these institutions is education, where the government finances the cost of providing the young with the essential skills for serving in the economy as workers. Before the institution of universal public education, worker skills were most often learned solely on the job. Another important primary institution is the social-insurance system, usually called social security, which aims at protecting workers and their families from want in times of the injury, disability, death, or unemployment of the family breadwinner, as well as against his obsolescence in old age.

The second form of welfare-state institutions consists of the residual institutions designed to help those at the very bottom of the stratification system. They include public assistance or welfare, and public housing. Because they serve only the poorest element of the population, their benefits are provided selectively, only where there is demonstrated need in terms of low income. In the original conception of the welfare state, it was envisioned that these residual institutions would become less and less necessary, and that the primary universal institutions would produce sufficient support to both reduce inequality and protect against poverty. The rediscovery of poverty in the 1960's has led, however, to a reassessment of the welfare-state model.

This rediscovery led to a new discussion of ways to end poverty and reduce inequalities. Three divergent strategies emerged from the involvement of the Federal government in the poverty arena. Each strategy was based upon different theories to explain why poverty still persists in an affluent welfare state. The first strategy was the service strategy, based upon the notion that the problem of poverty was a result of the characteristics of persons who were poor. The second strategy, based upon the premise that the primary problem of the poor was their need for money, held that with an adequate income they could be integrated into the economic structure at least in terms of consumption, if not production.[3] Thirdly, the power strategists placed the problem of poverty in the fact that the poor were powerless to effectively promote their interests; they were therefore unable to bring about the political and economic changes necessary to improve their circumstances.

THE SERVICE STRATEGY

The service strategy was the key to antipoverty programs of the 1960's. It is aimed at fitting poor people into the economic structure by changing the poor themselves. Theoretically, the fault for poverty lay in the characteristics of the people. One view was that there existed a "culture of poverty," a vicious cycle of despair and apathy, together with low motivation and lack of ability to seize opportunities for economic advancement. A less demeaning view, perhaps, was the notion that the poor lacked such characteristics as job skills and education, both of which were viewed as crucial for economic success. This lack was attributed to the absence of opportunities for the poor to gain the training necessary to compete favorably in today's sophisticated labor markets. In both the culture-of-poverty and lack-of-skills models, however, the key was to increase opportunities via people-changing policies, either in terms of modifying attitudes and motivation, or in terms of improving education and skills. For example, many of the service-strategy programs, notably in the area of job training, tried both to improve attitudes toward work and to increase skills and education, thereby increasing opportunity.

This service strategy relies almost entirely on residual institutions,[4] which were created and designed to serve only those clients who were screened on the basis of income. One key institution in this strategy is public assistance. Public-assistance agencies were charged by Congress, in the 1962 Public Welfare Amendments to the Social Security Act, with the responsibility for rehabilitating welfare recipients, especially those receiving Aid to Families with Dependent Children (AFDC). Congress bought the service strategy under the assumption that such services would result in a greater capacity for self-support and a corresponding lowering of the numbers on the welfare rolls. The legislative mandate was broad, however, and included services to promote "self-care" and "strengthen family life." This strategy, which focused upon personal services such as family counseling, carried the assumption that the poor were incompetent to manage their own affairs. Other more tangible services were also added, including educational projects, day care, and job counseling and training. The 1967 Amendments to the Social Security Act took up the "self-supporting" goal with a vengeance through the institution of the Work Incentive Program (WIN), which was renamed the WHIP program by welfare mothers. Refusal to accept a job or job training resulted in a cut in the cash grant. This forced training and work principle was again endorsed in the Talmadge Amendments of December, 1971. Here, the only mothers exempt from the work requirement were those with children under six years of age or mothers in families in which an adult male relative was eligible, registered for, and willing to accept training.

In addition to the above services provided for in the amendments to the Social Security Act, a new residual set of institutions to service the poor was set up following the Economic Opportunity Act of 1964. One of the focuses of this declared War on Poverty was upon the creation of opportunities through special education and training programs designed for, and perhaps by, the poor. These programs included Head Start for preschoolers, the Neighborhood Youth Corps and the Job Corps for adolescents and young adults, Work Experience and Training for adults, and provisions for day care. In addition, the Community Action Programs (CAP) were to mobilize and co-ordinate the delivery of such services to the poor. The Manpower Development and Training Act of 1962 was yet another piece of legislation of the service strategy. Following the declaration of the War on Poverty, this program was reoriented toward providing education and training for poor adults.

This much-criticized service strategy has now been declared bankrupt by President Nixon, who reiterated what radical critics had long been saying: Much of the monies invested in these programs pays the salaries of the welfare and service professionals. It certainly is time to reconsider a service strategy based upon a culture of poverty, or even people-changing policies. These attempts to change the poor so they fit into the system have not created a society which is more equal in 1970 than it was in 1960, before these service strategies were implemented.

THE INCOME STRATEGY

Critics of the service strategy have continually pointed out that what the poor really need in order to improve their economic position is more money. The poor, the argument goes, need a greater opportunity to compete for the goods and services that are generally provided in our society. For this they need money to purchase those goods and services. In addition there are specific programs which, although they involve the provision of services, actually have the effect of stretching the incomes of the poor. These services, including housing, health, and food programs, will therefore be discussed in terms of the income strategy. Some observers, however, would argue that these services should be replaced by outright cash grants.[5]

The largest income-strategy program is the social-insurance component of the 1935 Social Security Act, much amended and extended since its enactment. This is a primary universal program of Old Age, Survivors, Disability, and Health Insurance (OASDHI) and Unemployment Insurance. The drawback with this program is that it performs better as a mechanism to protect the nonpoor from falling into poverty than as an antipoverty device. The residual component of the Social Security Act is the much-criticized public-assistance program of welfare, which serves only the poor. Even then, only about one-fifth of the aggregate income of all poor families comes from this program. Furthermore, cash grants often involve an implicit requirement that the recipient also accept the welfare services which were outlined under the service strategy. The problems with this program and proposed reforms are discussed further in the next chapter.

In the area of health care, it is often the case that free provision of the service is a more than adequate substitute for extra income with which to pay for that service. It is very difficult to gauge a level of income which would adequately take care of everyone's health needs, since these needs vary from family to family. Thus, a health-care delivery system, in which part or all of the costs are borne collectively or publicly, makes good sense. In addition, since the health-care needs of the poor are often very high, the public provision of health care is an indirect way of redistributing resources to those who need them most. Public acceptance of part of the very high health-care burden which falls upon the aged has now been incorporated into the Social Security (social-insurance component) program in the 1965 amendments to the Social Security Act, which created Medicare. In these same amendments provisions were also made for medical assistance to the needy. This residual program, Medicaid, is included in the public-assistance component of the Social Security Act.

While it has been true, especially in large cities, that free public health care has been available for the poor as long as there have been public hospitals, the quality of such care has been notoriously inadequate. Programs like Medicare and Medicaid enable poor persons to use the higher-quality private health-care market without paying the full price. In addition, the Office of Economic Opportunity (OEO) entered the business of providing health care for the poor beginning in 1965. A major part of OEO's health-care budget goes for neighborhood health centers which provide services directly and are reimbursed for treating Medicare and Medicaid patients.[6] None of these programs, however, has yet solved the problem of providing adequate health care for all of the poor.[7]

Housing programs provided from governmental sources also may serve the function of reducing the amount of money low-income persons need spend to provide for their wants. Housing subsidies come in a variety of forms, including publicly provided housing, rent supplements, mortgage insurance, and the granting of loans at below-market interest rates. The programs that affect most Americans benefit middle-income persons almost exclusively, however. These are the mortgage-insurance programs administered by the Federal Housing Administration and the Veterans Administration, which are used to finance almost one-sixth of the nation's homes. Programs that aid the poor, on the other hand, aid less than 3 per cent of the population. Just over 1 per cent of the population resides in public housing, and under 2 per cent receive benefits from the other programs that have been developed. Thus, the vast majority of low-income persons are dependent upon the private-housing market, paying rents that often amount to 35 per cent of their income, often for apartments that are overcrowded, unsafe, and inadequately maintained.

Publicly assisted programs of housing construction for low-income persons were rapidly expanded following the Housing Act of 1968, but they required, in most cases, the participation and cooperation of local builders and political elites. The result was a massive expenditure of funds that often lined the pockets of corrupt builders and officials and produced shoddy housing. In 1972, President Nixon placed an eighteen-month freeze on new spending for housing assistance, and the future of publicly assisted low-income housing is very much in doubt.

The third set of programs which puts the equivalent of cash into the hands of poor persons is the group of food programs. The free school-lunch program for poor children is often not put into effect because schools in poor neighborhoods either cannot afford the local contribution which is required or they do not have kitchen facilities. Of greater overall impact are the two Department of Agriculture programs: food stamps and surplus commodities. The food-stamp program allows poor individuals and families to stretch their food dollars, but only if they spend a fairly high percentage of their total income on food. For this reason, very poor families often cannot afford to purchase food stamps. The second program involves the distribution of free surplus foods. This program, it has been suggested, is designed more for the farmer to unload his surplus crop than to satisfy the nutritional needs of poor families. For example, with the rapid food-price rises of early 1973, the Department of Agriculture discontinued the purchase of powdered milk for the surplus-food program. Furthermore, although these food programs do permit the poor to stretch their food dollars, this sort of provision "in kind," as opposed to "in cash," implies that the poor might not spend their money wisely if they were simply given cash rather than food stamps or free surplus foods. In the second version of President Nixon's Family Assistance Plan, he proposed to change this by the elimination of the Department of Agriculture's food programs and a subsequent increase in the income floor for a family of four from $1,600 to $2,400.

THE POWER STRATEGY

While the service strategy sees the solution to the problem of poverty in changing certain characteristics of the poor, and the income strategy sees the answer in providing money for the poor, the power strategy views the primary solution in obtaining greater power for the poor. In one sense, the power strategy is inherent in the American way: Immigrant groups who arrived poor and penniless were able to organize politically and achieve power, or at least a share of the power, in the major cities of the Northeast, and through a system of ward politics and patronage to move up in the stratification system. The tradition of citizen participation and local community control is, moreover, central to American democratic ideals. Somehow, the contemporary poor had been excluded from sharing in this process, either because of apathy or stigma, or the unwillingness of those who had already achieved power to share it.

The power strategy was put into effect in some of OEO's Community Action Programs. This came about as an unintended consequence of the rather vague requirement in the 1964 Economic Opportunity Act that there be "maximum feasible participation of residents of areas and members of the groups served." [8] The community action program was to be a flexible program involving the participation of the poor. Nevertheless, the exact meaning of such participation was left unclear in the original legislation and was probably also foggy in the minds of its supporters. As these programs began to be implemented, however, the power strategy became a popular interpretation among poor and middle-class radicals. Greater political power for the poor was to be achieved by organizing them into a politically effective power bloc which could then demand recognition by the local power coalition. One community-action program, in fact, identified its goal explicitly in terms of the power strategy: "to help low-income people to create powerful, autonomous democratic organization." [9] The program was interpreted to be a "grass-roots" program, unbeholden to either the established political leaders or the local power structure.

Not surprisingly, the power strategy was short-lived even in those places, such as large cities, where it did gain a foothold. It did not take long for local political leaders to perceive the threat to their power brought about by this new organization of poor persons. One local observer of a power-strategy program put it this way: "They are looking at poor people as a class—poor people rising as a class. . . . If you're talking about a mass program, you're saying, 'How do you galvanize the poor to break down the walls of the City?' " [10] At the 1965 Conference of Mayors it was pointed out that this sort of strategy involved class conflict and was therefore clearly Marxist and un-American.[11] Thus, the end of the power strategy came with the 1967 Green Amendment, which put local community-action programs firmly under the authority of the local government. Poor persons could remain as representatives on local community action boards, but, as Mrs. Green put it, "those who are helping to pay shall have a voice through the elected officials." [12] The poor, who can little afford to fund their own political organizations, were left impotent in the poverty coalition. The Community Action Programs ceased to be controversial.

One specific OEO program has also included some power-strategy action. This is the legal services program, designed to challenge the law or its implementation where it did not serve the best interests of the poor. As with the power strategy in the community-action programs, the power strategy of legal services was not fully carried out. "Class action" suits, brought by one party in the name of an aggrieved population category, represent a basic challenge to institutions maintaining poverty, but, nevertheless, have constituted only about 7 per cent of the total legal-services caseload.[13] This is probably due in part to the overwhelming need among the poor for legal help on individual matters as well as to the opposition to such class-action suits by government agencies which might be subject to their challenges. Nevertheless, a few notable suits have been successful in changing the power relations between the poor and the rest of the society. The most important examples come from California, where the California Rural Legal Assistance was able both to stop Governor Reagan's proposed cuts in the Medicaid program and to force the United States Department of Labor to cut back in its plans to import Mexican labor, which would have lowered the wages and incomes of American farm laborers.[14]

President Nixon's attempt to restrict the scope of legal services is a testimony to the success of this program in challenging the government to take into account the interests of the poor. Critics point to the absurdity of government-funded lawyers challenging governmental agencies. This, of course, is what the power strategy for the poor is all about. The power aspect of the legal services program, however, is in danger of being restricted, if not eliminated altogether.

THE JOB STRATEGY

This strategy is oriented toward reducing poverty and inequality through direct intervention in the labor market itself, in order to provide jobs at adequate wages. The incomes of the poor would be improved through the traditional economic institutions upon which the vast majority of individuals and families in the society gain their livelihood. The emphasis is upon modifying the present operation of the labor market in order to guarantee jobs at adequate wages for all who want them. The relevant policies require system-changing programs rather than people-changing programs, such as are the basis of the service strategy. These system-changing programs also imply more direct intervention in the market than does the income strategy.

The job strategy did not originate with the rediscovery of poverty in the 1960's. The first example of this type of policy is to be found in the Depression programs which provided work rather than relief for the unemployed. In 1935 these programs were placed under the direction of the Works Progress Administration (WPA). Continuing concern with the problem of unemployment prompted passage of the Employment Act of 1946, which set "full employment" as a goal to be achieved in American society.

The goal of full employment, however, has never been fully implemented. Rather, in recent years it has been allowed to wither away under the pressure of inflation as a result of the "trade-off" between inflation and unemployment. In practice, this trade-off means that once inflation becomes a problem, the level of "tolerable" unemployment is allowed to rise. Since the poor suffer most in times of high unemployment, this mechanism to combat inflation results in a further increase in inequality.[15] Concern with this trade-off has led to a curious logic of declaring a 4.5 per cent unemployment rate to be in fact "full employment." [16] In reality, in recent decades actual full employment—that is, an unemployment rate of less than 1 per cent, and that figure consisting only of individuals temporarily between jobs—has been achieved only under the tremendous economic pressures of World War II. In the postwar years, the government has been reluctant to intervene in order to lower unemployment rates, except by the rather questionable method of providing tax cuts for industry.

In addition to job creation and full employment, a third aspect of the job-strategy policy is one of establishing minimum wages. The impetus for this program, too, came from the experience of the Depression. The first national minimum wage legislation to be upheld by the Supreme Court was included in the Fair Labor Standards Act of 1938. The goal of this legislation was to provide every worker with at least "the minimum standard of living necessary for health, efficiency and general well-being." [17] As an antipoverty device, however, this program, as currently implemented, has two serious drawbacks. The first is that many workers receive less than the legal minimum wage. This is due partly to the fact that the legislation is not systematically enforced, and partly to the fact that certain types of workers, like domestic servants and employees of small firms in trade and industry, are not covered by this legal minimum. The second drawback is that a family of four headed by a worker earning the minimum wage full-year for full-time work in 1972 still would be in poverty, as defined by the Social Security Administration, if no additional income were received.[18]

One objection often made to this "solution" to the problem of low wages is that if the minimum wage were to be strictly enforced and raised sufficiently to bring a breadwinner's family of four out of poverty, then the number of jobs available to the poor would decrease. Unemployment would thereby increase, and the poor might be, in fact, worse off.[19] An alternative method of raising low wages is for the government to provide a wage subsidy to supplement the wages of very low earners. A cash-transfer program, this would be an income strategy, rather than a job strategy, although it would obviously encourage the poor to accept low-wage work. One recent proposal along these lines is the negative wage tax.[20]

Antipoverty programs of the 1960's did not focus upon the job strategy. Even the programs designed to help individuals obtain greater income from work were oriented toward job training (people-changing policies), which fit into the service strategy, not the job strategy. Two Office of Economic Opportunity programs, however, did create jobs. One was the Neighborhood Youth Corps, which supplied jobs for teenagers; the other was the Work Experience and Training program, which provided work for welfare recipients. Later, a New Careers program to employ professional aides as intermediates between the service professionals and the poor was created in addition to jobs in community beautification. The overall impact of these job-creation programs in the War on Poverty, however, was slight.

The War on Poverty did lead to a discovery of the working poor, where full-year full-time work resulted in a below-poverty level of living for the worker and his family. A subemployment index was developed to measure the extent of unemployment, involuntary part-time employment, and full-time year-round employment at poverty wages. High subemployment rates, especially in urban slums, forced policy makers to re-examine the possibilities of the job strategy. Consequently, the emphasis of the Manpower Development and Training Act of 1962 shifted from job training classes to on-the-job training (OJT). By subsidizing private industry to hire and train the hard-core unemployed, the government hoped to create new job opportunities for the subemployed. These programs, however, cannot be counted as victories in a war on either poverty or inequality. The conclusion of the General Accounting Office was rather that:

OJT Contracts had served primarily to reimburse employers for OJT which they would have conducted even without the Government's financial assistance. These contracts were awarded even though the intent of the program was to induce *new* or *additional training efforts* beyond those usually carried out.[21]

In contrast to the poor, employers received a substantial benefit from these programs; sixty million dollars was given to the National Alliance of Businessmen to hire and train the hard core in the JOBS program in 1968.[22]

Some critics of the War on Poverty have suggested that the government itself should guarantee a job at adequate wages for every citizen who wants to work, by becoming the employer of last resort. Individuals who could not obtain an adequately paying job in the private sector could then apply for a job with the government, which would be required to provide them with jobs. According to a 1969 opinion poll, such a strategy would receive the support of approximately 64 per cent of American adults.[23] Nevertheless, this is not the direction envisaged by the Nixon Administration. George Schultz, then Secretary of Labor, indicated the administration's position in a discussion of Nixon's proposed Family Assistance Plan (FAP):

... the labor market itself must be recognized as a constraint on the full achievement of our expectations. It is a fact that our economy has a lot of jobs that pay low wages, and we are not going to be remaking the economy in this program. We have to relate to the labor market. We can only put people in the jobs that exist.[24]

Any discussion of the job strategy in terms of reducing poverty and inequality must eventually confront the basic problem posed by the fact that in our economy some workers receive very high wages while others are paid very low ones. This phenomenon of inequality in the distribution of wages has yet to be fully understood. In order for the job strategy to be successful in reducing both poverty and inequality, however, it will be important to understand this process of wage differentiation.

Classical economic theory states that a worker is paid according to how much his work contributes to the overall productivity of the firm; each worker is paid according to his "net marginal productivity." According to this theory, the foreman who makes seven dollars an hour is more productive than the assembly-line worker who makes four dollars an hour. By the same token, the lunch-counter waitress who makes two dollars per hour is less productive than the cocktail waitress who makes nine dollars per hour. The problem remains as to what the precise meaning of "productivity" actually is.

In the early 1960's economists thought that they had found the key to a worker's productivity in his educational attainment.[25] Thus, they argued, the higher the education, the higher the productivity and, consequently, the higher the wages. Antipoverty programs based upon increasing the education of poor persons would be justified by this theory. Recent research indicates, however, that educational differences cannot explain differences in economic success. Once the socioeconomic background of the individual is taken into account, neither education nor I.Q. contributes much in determining income.[26] Furthermore, while differences in educational attainment have narrowed considerably in the postwar period, differences in income have not.[27]

An alternate theory of wage differentials suggests that a hierarchy of wages is created by employers as a means of maintaining authority and discipline. Supervisory workers are always paid more than individuals who work under them, even where this violates notions of productivity and market value. It may be, as Barbara Wootton has suggested, that differences in wages reflect traditional notions of status, in the society.[28] Thus, white-collar workers, who have high status, are traditionally paid more than blue-collar workers, who have low status irrespective of the "productivity" of either. Women and Blacks, who have low status, generally receive lower wages than equally trained and qualified men and Whites, whose overall status in the society is higher.

A third theory of wage differentials suggests that these are the result of differential rates of development in different sectors of the economy. In the rich corporate sector profits are such that employers can afford to pay higher wages, while in marginal industries such as clothing and the services (for example, laundry service), profits, like wages, are low. Thus, a worker performing the same kind of work will make perhaps twice as much if he is in the steel industry than if he were in the clothing industry. This uneven development, which some view as inherent in capitalism,[29] results from the fact that industries with higher profits can reinvest in order to further improve their productivity. Moreover, they benefit from tax savings provided for them by government and are able to pay lobbyists to convince congressmen to vote in accordance with the corporation's interest on future legislation. This theory of wage differentials views the problem of poverty as one in which the poor are trapped in the low-wage, marginal industrial sector, with little chance to obtain a higher paying job in the rich corporate sector.

Thus far, none of these theories has been tested sufficiently against reality to yield a clear explanation of the great inequalities in the wages of workers. Such an understanding, however, would be necessary for a full-fledged pursuit of the job strategy. Nevertheless, it is clear that the job strategy does suggest a radical reorientation toward governmental intervention in the labor market. It implies that the government ought to be responsible for system changes that would create a society in which everyone who wanted to work could get a job at adequate wages. Furthermore, exorbitant wages such as the six-figure salary of the president of the bankrupt Penn Central Railroad would no longer be viewed as justifiable in this society. It is for these reasons that the service and income strategies, at least in their more modest forms, have been more popular among government policy makers in the decade of the 1960's. Whether there will develop any effective strategy of poverty or inequality reform in the 1970's is as yet in doubt. In his first term, President Nixon demonstrated a preference for an income strategy over a service strategy. Since his very modest Family Assistance Plan (to be discussed in the next chapter) failed to pass Congress in 1972, however, he apparently has abandoned all pursuit of any strategies of poverty reduction, and has never demonstrated any interest in reducing inequality.

1. See T. H. Marshall, *Citizenship and Social Class* (London: Cambridge University Press, 1950), pp. 91–106.

2. For a description of the residual concept of social welfare, see Harold L. Wilensky and Charles N. Lebeaux, *Industrial Society and Social Welfare* (New York: The Free Press, 1965), pp. 138ff.

3. See Lee Rainwater, "The Service Strategy vs. the Income Strategy," *Transaction* (October 1967), pp. 40–41, for another, and somewhat different definition of these two approaches.

4. The key primary institution involved in the service strategy is education. Here Title 1 of the Elementary and Secondary Education Act of

1965 attempted to provide extra help for educating children of low-income families.

5. Rainwater, *op. cit.*, pp. 40–41.

6. Sar A. Levitan, *The Great Society's Poor Law* (Baltimore: The Johns Hopkins Press, 1969), pp. 192ff.

7. In addition to the above programs the Veterans Administration provides pensions and compensation as well as medical care for those who qualify.

8. Office of Economic Opportunity, *Economic Opportunity Act of 1964, as Amended* (Washington, D.C., 1966), p. 14.

9. Warren C. Haggstrom, "Who Fear the Poor" (mimeo, November 1967), p. 9.

10. Ben Zimmerman as quoted in Erwin Knoll and Jules Witcover, "Organizing the Poor," in Herman P. Miller, ed., *Poverty American Style* (Belmont, Calif.: Wadsworth Publishing Company, 1966), p. 248.

11. See Michael Harrington, *The Politics of Poverty* (New York: League for Industrial Democracy, 1965), p. 18.

12. Quoted in *The New York Times*, November 8, 1967.

13. Levitan, *op. cit.*, p. 186.

14. Discussed in *ibid.*, pp. 186–87.

15. See Robinson G. Hollister and John L. Palmer, "The Implicit Tax of Inflation and Unemployment: Some Policy Implications," in Kenneth E. Boulding and Martin Pfaff, eds., *Redistribution to the Rich and the Poor* (Belmont, Calif.: Wadsworth Publishing Company, 1972), pp. 369–373.

16. T. Aldrich Finegan, "Labor Force Growth and the Return to Full Employment," *Monthly Labor Review*, 95 (February 1972), p. 29.

17. Quoted in Clair Wilcox, *Toward Social Welfare* (Homewood, Ill.: Richard D. Irwin, 1969), p. 214.

18. In 1972 the Federal minimum wage was $1.60 per hour. An individual who worked forty hours a week for fifty-two weeks would have earned only $3,328 for the year, a figure considerably below the poverty line, which was $4,137 for a family of four in 1971.

19. See Wilcox, *op. cit.*, p. 225.

20. Edgar K. Browning, "Alternative Programs for Income Redistribution: the NIT and the NWT," *American Economic Review* (March 1973), pp. 38–49.

21. Quoted in Howard M. Wachtel, "Looking at Poverty from a Radical Perspective," *Review of Radical Political Economics*, 3 (Summer 1971), p. 13.

22. *Ibid.*, p. 13.

23. See Joe R. Feagin, "Poverty: We Still Believe that God Helps Those Who Help Themselves," *Psychology Today*, 6 (November 1972), p. 108.

24. George P. Schultz, "The Nixon Welfare Plan," *New Generation,* 52 (Winter 1970), p. 8.

25. See Gary S. Becker, *Human Capital* (New York: Columbia University Press, 1964).

26. Samuel Bowles and Herbert Gintis, "I.Q. in the U.S. Class Structure," *Social Policy* (January/February 1973), pp. 70–73.

27. See Robinson Hollister, "Education and the Distribution of Income: Some Exploratory Forays," in *Education and Distribution of Income, VII* (Paris: Organization for Economic Co-operation and Development, 1971), p. 16.

28. Barbara Wootton, *The Social Foundations of Wage Policy* (London: Allen and Unwin, 1955).

29. See Barry Bluestone, "Capitalism and Poverty in America," *Monthly Review*, 24 (June 1962), p. 68; and Bluestone, "The Tripartite Economy: Labor Markets and the Working Poor," *Poverty and Human Resources*, 5 (July–August 1970), pp. 24–25.

8
Cash-Transfer Programs and the Reduction of Inequality

Sally Bould Van Til

One important mechanism by which a more equal society can be created is through the redistribution of income. Inequalities in the original distribution of income on the basis of wages (labor), interest (capital), and rent (land) can be lessened by redistributing income through the use of a progressive tax system combined with a system of cash transfers. This form of creating a more equal society is often viewed, especially by taxpayers, as taking from the rich via taxes and giving to the poor via cash transfers. Politicians tend to shrink from the notion of "soaking the rich" in order to provide for the poor. Thus, the creation of a more equal distribution of income has not been a goal of cash-transfer programs in the United States. It is not surprising, therefore, that over half such transfers and publicly subsidized fringe benefits in the United States go into the pockets of the nonpoor,[1] that is, families whose pretransfer income was already above the Social Security Administration's poverty line.

The historical experience of cash transfers in the United States points to the fact that we entered late and timidly into these programs, relative to other industrialized Western nations. The pressure of the Great Depression in the 1930's prompted a substantial shift away from an often haphazard system of private charities, state and local relief (often in the form of donations of food and clothing), and the system of poorhouses or almshouses which had been the nineteenth-century solution to the problem of poverty. The Social Security Act of 1935, which was passed in response to the conditions of the 1930's, marked the beginning of the Federal government's direct involvement with cash transfers on a large scale. This legislation, as amended, still remains the primary program of direct cash transfers in the United States. The intention of this legislation, however, was not primarily one of redistribution, in terms of reducing income inequalities between the rich and the poor; nor was it even primarily aimed at the reduction or alleviation of poverty. The goal of the program is perhaps best embodied in the concluding statement of the Committee on Economic Security's 1935 report:

The program will promote social and industrial stability and will operate to enlarge and make steady a widely diffused purchasing power upon which depends the high American standard of living and the internal market for our mass production, industry and agriculture.[2]

The 1935 legislation created a broad-based social security program, including two distinct parts: the "social-insurance" components of Old Age Insurance, or "social security," and the Unemployment Insurance program; and the "assistance" component, which is technically "Public Assistance" or "welfare." [3] The primary program was to be the social-insurance component, while the public-assistance component was to be only a stop-gap program designed to wither away as more and more individuals came to be covered by social insurance.

The first of the two parts, the social-insurance component, was based upon the philosophy of private insurance: that is, sharing risks by pooling resources over large numbers of individuals who contribute to the scheme and thus receive a benefit as of *right*. Such a program had obvious appeal to those who wanted to preserve some of the old-fashioned "rugged individualism," with the government, instead of the private sector, running the program on a "compulsory" basis. At the same time, moreover, the benefit would reflect a contribution, making is possible to do away with the obnoxious means test, which required public prying into the private financial affairs of families and individuals.

This system of "social insurance" was intended to protect individuals and families from the primary risks that very often resulted in falling into poverty. These were identified as old age, unemployment, disability, and death of the breadwinner.[4] The occurrence of any one of these conditions usually resulted in the loss of earnings of the family breadwinner. To guard against these risks, every worker would be required to contribute a portion of his earnings into a scheme from which he could draw a benefit (i.e., a social security check) as of right when he was victim of one of the above "risks."[5] Thus, he and his family would be protected from falling into poverty. In an effort to keep to the private insurance model as closely as possible, benefits were related to contributions and, hence, to previous earnings upon which the beneficiary had paid his social security tax.

With the advantage of hindsight, it is clear that the social-insurance component, the primary component of the Social Security Act, was also designed to assure a stable attachment to the work force for those in working ages who were able-bodied. Thus, those individuals who had never worked, or worked only irregularly, would have earned little or no benefits for themselves or their families to be drawn upon during times of old age, unemployment, or widowhood.[6] In addition, the program was not designed to provide an above-poverty standard of living for those individuals who had lived below the poverty standard when the breadwinner was working. Therefore, such a program would not protect the working poor from being still poorer during times of unemployment, disability, and retirement. This problem has been alleviated, in part, by increasing the minimum benefit for low-wage earners. While this mechanism does redistribute some of the social-security social-insurance funds from high earners to low earners, it is counterbalanced by the fact that the worker's contribution, or social security tax, is a regressive tax on earnings. In other words, low earners pay a higher proportion of their earnings into the social security fund than high earners.[7]

The public-assistance component of the Social Security Act was patterned after the social-insurance component in that it identified specific categories in which the risk of poverty was high and then created programs which would provide cash assistance on the basis of a test of means to needy persons in those categories. This program was to tide over persons in real need until the social security system could become fully operational. Thus the programs of Old Age Assistance, Aid to the Blind, and Aid to the Permanently and Totally Disabled were designed to help these groups. Similarly, the Aid to Dependent Children program—now Aid to Families with Dependent Children (AFDC)—was to replace the older program of mothers' pensions which protected children primarily in cases where the breadwinner was deceased. The original AFDC program, too, was intended primarily for widows, but gradually began to cover more and more recipients in other categories of single mothers[8]—i.e., divorced, separated, deserted, and unwed.

Instead of withering away, as the founders of the social security system had predicted, this component has grown; the total number of recipients of all Federal public-assistance programs increased almost threefold from 1950 to 1971.[9] The rate of growth has been most rapid in the past five years, resulting in the term "Crisis in Welfare."[10] More specifically, it has been the public-assistance program for families with dependent children (AFDC) where growth has been most dramatic. Rapid growth has also occurred in the public-assistance program for the permanently and totally disabled, while the numbers on Old Age Assistance and Aid to the Blind have decreased somewhat since 1950.

The welfare crisis resulted in a broad-based concern for welfare reform. In the 1960's three distinct constituencies emerged, each supporting a different avenue for reform.[11] The first constituency is composed of the old guard of the social-insurance movement, who claim that the original act never went far enough, especially in the areas of health insurance, temporary sickness and disability insurance, and children's allowances. Thus, the costs of sickness and disability and bringing up a child were left uncovered by the American social-insurance component, leaving the public-assistance component, and especially the AFDC program, to fill in the gap. The precedent for extending the social-insurance component into areas such as health, temporary disability, and children's allowances could be found in the actions of most other industrialized nations. The argument for children's allowances, which provide a cash grant for all children covered by the program irrespective of need, could easily be made by pointing out the high degree of child poverty in America. In addition, new risks such as the risk of divorce, desertion, and separation might be covered; this was the goal of Alvin Schorr's proposal to provide against the risk of falling into poverty due to family breakup.[12]

The second important constituency in the welfare-reform movement of the 1960's was composed primarily of public-assistance bureaucrats and welfare professionals. This group focused, not surprisingly, upon reforming and federalizing the public-assistance component. Currently, the states must supply 35 to 50 per cent of the costs of the cash grant beyond a certain minimum and pay for half of their administrative costs. The proposal for the Federal government to pick up the entire cost was popular in the Northern states where the pinch of large welfare budgets was being felt. Furthermore, such a reform might at least bring more equity into a system which paid the average family on AFDC in New York the sum of $288 per month in 1971 while the average family in Mississippi received only $55 per month during the same year.[13] With the Federal government in charge and paying the full cost, it was also hoped that some reasonable national minimum standards might be established—a procedure which the Southern states had successfully kept out of the original legislation.

In addition to reforming the cash programs of public assistance, however, the welfare professionals stressed the delivery of services along with the cash payments. Their goal was to pursue an income strategy in conjunction with a service strategy. The latter, as indicated in Chapter 7, was to enable problem families to overcome their problems, to become more self-sufficient, and ultimately to be self-supporting. Congress bought the argument that such services would help reduce the welfare rolls. The Federal government now supports 75 per cent of the costs of specified social services which are delivered by local public-assistance professionals.

The third constituency for welfare reform is dominated by economists who want to integrate a system of cash transfers for the poor directly into the income-tax structure. The implication here is that the total picture of who pays and who benefits should be examined. Proponents argue, therefore, that both the tax system and the form of the cash transfer should be evaluated together. It has long been recognized that our system of tax deductions benefits the nonpoor but not the poor. If a family has little or no income the value of such deductions is zero or close to zero, whereas for a family with a large income the value of the income-tax deduction may be considerable. One simple solution is to provide the value of such deductions to poor families by simply giving them the amount of their deductions in cash. Under this system each family would report its income to the Internal Revenue Service at regular intervals. If the income was above standard, taxes would be paid in the conventional fashion. If, on the other hand, the income level of the family fell below standard, a direct cash payment would be made to the family. The payment would vary with the difference between earned income and an accepted standard. Thus the name "negative" income tax—which means a direct payment to families and individuals whose incomes are below this standard.[14]

This negative-income-tax approach would avoid certain flaws in the current public-assistance programs. First, it would provide a floor of income for all families and individuals in the society. Second, it would establish a "right" to such a minimum income floor similar to the right to tax exemptions and deductions. Third, it would reduce the bureaucratic costs and the stigmatizing effects of the current prying into the financial means of the family or individual household; income simply could be declared and the Internal Revenue Service could make spot checks as it now does for payers of the "positive" income tax. Fourth, it would be an efficient mechanism for delivering cash where it is most needed. And last, it would interfere as little as possible in the normal operations of the market. This last characteristic in particular has great appeal for economists, especially those who stress the benefits of a market free of governmental interference. Thus, it is not surprising that the first proponent of a negative-income-tax approach was the conservative economist Milton Friedman.[15]

Under the negative income tax, families with no income would be supported at the basic income floor below which no one would fall; beyond that point a fraction of all earned income would be taxed. In Friedman's proposed negative income tax the floor was set at $1,500 for a family of four with a "marginal tax rate" of 50 percent; a family earning no outside income would receive a minimum guarantee of $1,500, a family earning $2,000 would end up with $2,500 (the $1,500 guarantee and half of the earned $2,000), and the family earning $3,000 would "break even"—ending the year with $3,000 (the $1,500 guarantee plus half the earned income).[16] All families earning more than $3,000 would pay taxes in the conventional way—that is "positive" taxes.

One important characteristic of the negative income tax is that the family which earns income from work will always be better off than the family of the same size which has no income from work. Thus, the "economic"[17] incentive to work is preserved. The degree of economic incentive, however, is determined by the marginal tax rate. In Friedman's example the marginal tax rate of 50 per cent would provide a greater economic incentive to work than one of 75 per cent but less than one of 25 per cent. Friedman's proposal allows the family to keep fifty cents of every additional dollar earned, while a rate of 75 per cent would allow the family to keep only twenty-five cents, and a rate of 25 per cent would allow the family to keep seventy-five cents of each additional dollar earned.

In this manner, "equity" or fairness by the test of the market value of work has been preserved, while inequality has been reduced. The higher the basic minimum provided, and the lower the "marginal tax rate," the more the inequality is reduced, and, of course, the more expensive the program becomes. Under all forms of the negative income tax, however, the "equity" problem is resolved by guaranteeing that, number of children held constant, the family that earns more income will end the year with more money than the family that earns less. What is at stake is the level of the minimum floor. Friedman tended to set the basic floor at a relatively low level, i.e., $1,500 for a family of four. Liberal economists such as Tobin and Lampman have proposed higher minimum floors, thereby making the program both more generous and more expensive.[18]

The three constituencies for these three variants of welfare reform have had varying success in seeing their programs enacted by Congress. The welfare professionals did achieve success in obtaining a program for service delivery in 1962; their proposals, supported by commission reports, for a fully federalized welfare system have been accepted in part by the reforms of 1972. The social security constituency could count among its gains the raising of the level of the minimum social security (OASDI) benefit and the extension of coverage in the OASDI program, together with the addition of a health component which resulted in a change of the name of the program to Old Age, Survivors, Disability and Health Insurance (OASDHI). In the area of negative income tax, bills have been proposed by Senators Harris and Ribicoff. But, in August of 1969, President Nixon preempted the strategies of these three constituencies in his proposal for a Family Assistance Plan (FAP).

The Family Assistance Plan (FAP) combined aspects of a federalized public-assistance program together with a negative-income-tax approach for poor families with children. It was a composite program which combined various elements in such a way as to please none of the three constituencies entirely. First, it was purely an income strategy which contained an implicit assumption, which has now been made explicit by President Nixon, of eliminating or greatly reducing the service strategy of the Kennedy-Johnson years. Needless to say, this did not please welfare professionals, as Moynihan has pointed out.[19] Second, although there was to be full Federal financing of the basic minimum, that minimum was so low—$1,600 plus food stamps for a family of four or $2,400 without food stamps—that it exceeded the minimum AFDC grant in only eleven states. There was no sign of relief, therefore, for Northern states with high AFDC grant levels.

The negative-income-tax constituency held a slightly more favorable view of FAP; the plan, however, fell far short of the ideal. First, it would, in effect, only add a new category to the present hodgepodge of programs—that being the group of working poor families with children. Thus, it would not build a minimum floor for all; families without children and single individuals would not be covered. Second, it became clear as the bill progressed through the Congress, that the administration of the plan would not be simple; fear of a lack of incentives to work led to a stringent work requirement to be enforced by local administrators. In the final version of FAP the official marginal tax rate was not low—67 per cent, meaning that recipients could keep only one-third of every dollar earned. When state and local taxes and the social security tax were also considered, there was not much "economic" incentive to work left; the work requirement was the result of this observation. With such a work requirement, moreover, there could be no clear "right" to assistance since receipt of the grant would depend upon the discretion of local administrators in determining who was employable and who must accept available jobs. In short, economists saw some gains in accepting the "principle" of a negative income tax, but that was about all.

The social-security constituency and Democrats in general took a less than enthusiastic view of the FAP program. A key reason for the latter's position was no doubt that it was a Republican program. The result was that there was no strong support from the groups who generally support such reforms. Nevertheless, the death of the FAP program in the fall of 1972 can be attributed as much if not more to the fierce conservative opposition as to the generally lukewarm liberal support. With the death of FAP, welfare reformers returned to the drawing boards and the discussion of the pros and cons of various proposals will no doubt continue for some time before any substantial congressional action is taken. The following discussion will attempt to outline the important elements of this continuing debate over various income-maintenance programs and to examine two very critical dimensions and their related implications.

The first dimension is whether the program is to be categorical. In other words, is the program to be directed at certain groups among the population to the exclusion of other groups? Will membership in a particular group, such as children or the aged, be required in order to be a beneficiary of such programs? A noncategorical program, on the other hand, is available to everyone regardless of age, sex, family, or work status, and every member of the community is treated equally with respect to his rights to benefit under the system.

Second, there is the question of whether the program will be means-tested or income-tested, or whether instead it will be granted to everyone regardless of income. This element, of course, has to do with efficiency. That is, the greater the proportion of the total outlay for cash transfers which actually reaches the poor, the more efficient the program is. A means-tested program is more efficient since nearly all of the money spent is received by the poor. In a nonmeans-tested program need is not a criteria for eligibility and benefits go to the poor and nonpoor alike. Nonmeans-tested programs tend to be inefficient because so much of the benefits are received by the nonpoor.

There are other issues related to means testing besides efficiency. One of the most important of these is stigma. The assumption here is that requiring an income test, especially a means test, for a program stigmatizes the recipients of that program as being low-income individuals. Further, to the extent that there is a stigma on poverty and dependency in society, individuals who apply for benefit from a program will thereby be labeled as poor and dependent persons. In addition, a means test is potentially a deterrent. Thus, a means-tested program rarely, if ever, reaches all those who are eligible to apply, in part because those individuals cannot be found, and in part because they are reluctant to announce publicly the fact of their low income.

In order, then, to examine the possibilities and to catalogue existing programs, these two dimensions—categorical vs. noncategorical, and means- or income-tested vs. nonmeans- or nonincome-tested—can be combined. This provides for an initial cataloguing of different income-maintenance proposals and programs which exist today. It is, of course, not meant as a complete catalogue. Nevertheless since these two dimensions, either in themselves or in their broader implications, reflect some of the most important issues in choice of income-maintenance programs, this cataloguing illustrates clearly the dimensions and potential choices which are involved, as well as the impact of the two dimensions as reflected in the programs.

In Box A of the diagram following are those means-tested programs which are categorical; that is, they are designed to help certain specific categories of eligible persons within the population, and they

	Categorical	Noncategorical
MEANS-TESTED	Public Assistance A	Negative Income Tax B
NONMEANS-TESTED	C OASDI Unemployment Insurance Children's Allowance	D Demogrant

are means-tested. An example of this program is the present Federal public-assistance program, which requires everywhere a test of means or at least, a declaration of income. This program reflects the kind of stigma that is attached to means-tested programs; a stigma which, in part, explains why public assistance is still underutilized even in an era of rising numbers on public relief. Only one-fifth of the aggregate income of poor families came from public assistance in 1970.[20]

Lack of sufficient income, however, is not the sole requirement for public-assistance eligibility. Applicants also must be able to fit into one of a number of classifications, such as Aid to the Blind, which is given to needy blind individuals, Aid to the Permanently and Totally Disabled, Aid to Families with Dependent Children, originally given only in cases where the dependent children's father was absent. Later the Congress found it amenable to propose an extended category to cover the situation where the father might be at home but unemployed. This program (AFDC-UP) has not been widely enacted.[21] Needy individuals falling outside of these categories cannot qualify for Federal public assistance. Thus, a lone individual who is neither aged, blind, nor disabled can only hope for help from the state and local General Assistance program. This program not only varies by state but also by counties within states; it is rarely a dependable source for even a minimum subsistence income for those who fail to qualify for one of the Federal programs.

In Box B of the diagram on page 113 are non-categorical programs which are means-tested. These programs, therefore, are open to everyone simply by virtue of proof of need, however that is defined. Need, then, is the sole criterion for availing oneself of these programs. The best known of these programs is the proposed negative income tax. The negative income tax, as put forth in different versions by Professors Friedman, Tobin, Lampman and Senators Harris and Ribicoff, is open to every member of the population simply on the basis of a lack of sufficient income.

In Boxes C and D are the nonmeans-tested income-maintenance programs. These are programs for which need is not an eligibility requirement. Again, these programs may be of one of two sorts, either categorical or noncategorical. In the noncategorical, nonmeans-tested program all members of the population are eligible for a benefit since there is no requirement on the basis of previous contributions, membership in a specific category, or need. This type of program is called a demogrant, which means simply a grant of money going to all members of the population. Dr. Eveline Burns of the Columbia School of Social Work advocated a demogrant scheme in the mid-1960's, and Senator George McGovern brought this program before the general public as a part of his initial campaign platform as a Presidential candidate in 1972.

The largest program now in existence is represented by Box C, a categorical program which is not means-tested. In this group are to be found all the income-maintenance programs of the social-insurance type under the general rubric of social security. This includes the OASDI (Old-Age Survivors and Disability Insurance) and Unemployment Insurance. A similar program, children's allowances, although not existent in the United States, is found in almost all other industrialized countries. In no case is there a means test, although in the OASDI program there is a limitation on earnings. In order to qualify for these programs, one must first fit one of the categories of either being aged, a child, disabled, widowed, or unemployed. In addition, eligibility also requires a financial participation in the program prior to the receipt of benefits. Such participation is open only to those who have been working in covered employment for a sufficient length of time, except that this is often not required for the receipt of children's allowances.

With the current interest by reformers focused upon the negative income tax, the concern of income-maintenance programs has completed a full circle from the nineteenth century. Poor laws in both England and the United States, in the nineteenth century, had the effect of accepting all the poor on the basis of the eligibility test, satisfied in most cases by entrance into the workhouse or the almshouse. Thus, the laws were, in effect, noncategorical. That is, all were accepted, and there was a very stringent, demeaning and odious test of need. Much has been written about conditions in these poorhouses or almshouses.

In the early part of this century, reformers in both England and the United States began to push for a "breakup of the poor law." These laws focused solely on the poor and resulted, so the reformers argued, in the poor being isolated and stigmatized by programs whose implementation tended to be harsh and often cruel. The alternative was to design programs to help everyone with problems known to be related to poverty rather than to design programs only to help poor people. The solution was the development of a number of categorical programs based upon these problem areas which would be available to all program participants in times of presumed need, but without the actual application of the obnoxious means test. The first group to be singled out in England for this kind of help was the aged, with the institution of the universal pension scheme in 1911. Not until the Social Security Act of 1935 were similar broad-based nonmeans-tested, categorical programs enacted in the United States.

With hindsight, it is now possible to direct two criticisms toward that particular approach, that is, the categorical, nonmeans-tested program embodied in our social security system. First of all, as was previously mentioned, in nonmeans-tested programs much of the money goes to those who are not poor. Thus, in 1961, 37 per cent of the OASDI beneficiaries were not poor before the cash transfers. Among Unemployment Insurance beneficiaries, 64 per cent were not poor before the transfer.[22] Estimates of children's allowance programs indicate that more than 80 per cent of the money would go to the nonpoor. Thus, such programs, it is argued, would be very inefficient, with only a small portion of the money going directly to the poor. Furthermore, such programs rarely solve the problem of poverty since many beneficiaries remain poor after receiving their benefit; in 1961 24 per cent of OASDI beneficiaries and 16 per cent of Unemployment Insurance beneficiaries were still poor.[23] To solve the problem of those who still remain poor would require higher benefit levels and higher social security taxes.

The most expensive form of program is the demogrant, which is noncategorical and goes to everyone irrespective of need. This characteristic was, of course, one of the things that the Republican campaigners immediately seized upon in criticizing George McGovern's proposal. They noted the enormous cost of his proposed demogrant of one thousand dollars per person per year. During the heated primary campaign in California Senator Humphrey charged that the cost of such a program would be approximately 72 billion dollars.[24] A more sober estimate of costs, however, must take into account the way in which the demogrant would be financed, a consideration to be discussed later.

The public-assistance cash programs are far more efficient than social security in terms of getting money to the poor.[25] Thus, in contrast to the OASDI and Unemployment Insurance beneficiaries, only 7 percent of the public assistance beneficiaries in 1961 were not poor before receiving the transfer.[26] Since the vast majority of public assistance cash transfers goes only to the poor, the costs of such a program are much less than programs which serve large numbers of nonpoor as well. This efficiency of public assistance in directly allocating money for the poor, however, must be weighed against the manner in which that efficiency is achieved. The mechanism which assures that only the poor receive the benefit is that of means-testing—i.e., requiring that the applicant prove that he is in fact poor. While the means test assures the society that its monies go only to the poor, the unavoidable result is that the poor are isolated and left prey to the stigma which modern society still attaches to the state of being poor.

The historical generalization that programs which serve only the poor invariably become programs of poor quality has a great deal of support. Such programs have been "poor" not only because they are inadequate but also because they have aroused the anger of the poor and the nonpoor alike. The poor have traditionally been very weak advocates in their own behalf, possessing the fewest resources for political influence in a democratic society. The nonpoor, both the working class and the middle class, view programs directed solely at the poor as an unfair burden in terms of their hard-earned tax dollars. The result is a stringent program which no one supports, least of all the poor, who must undergo a demeaning means-test in order to qualify for the often meager benefits. The cash grant is viewed as a privilege which is bestowed upon the poor by the nonpoor and not a rightful claim of the poor upon the society's resources. In times of rising relief rolls the image of welfare chiselers has always been politically popular. It is not surprising then, that under such a program large numbers of eligible poor persons fail to apply for benefits.

The nonmeans-tested social security program aimed to avoid these problems by providing for support from a broad-based political constituency. The continuous raises in social-security benefits together with the program's ability to withstand political attacks such as that from Senator Goldwater in 1964, indicate the success of the program in this area. Unlike the public-assistance program, moreover, almost all of those who are eligible do indeed apply and receive the benefits of the program. Nevertheless, success in building a political constituency has not resulted in success in dealing with the problems of poverty.

The negative income tax, a noncategorical but means-tested program, was viewed as a way to get around some of the dilemmas in the other programs. First, a simple declaration of income on a prepared form could replace the more detailed and personal means test presently used. Second, the Internal Revenue Service (IRS), a large, impersonal bureaucracy with its headquarters in Washington, D.C., could administer the program without the kinds of stigma and prying which often occur in the local administration by departments of public assistance. The IRS involvement would imply that the program also applied to the nonpoor and those paying the traditional "positive" income tax. Because nearly everyone fills out an income tax form, the problem of people not applying due to fear of stigma would be much less than under the current public-assistance programs. Third, because it is noncategorical, the negative income tax would apply to everyone in the society. Finally, because the program would be means-tested, cash assistance would go to those who need it most. Thus the program would be efficient.

There is one other problem implicit in the means-tested vs. nonmeans-tested dilemma, a problem that has plagued the development of any kind of redistributive program from the very conception of the idea. That is, what should be done about work incentives? Here again, the proponents of nonmeans-tested programs argue that their programs avoid this problem by giving the benefit to everyone, so that no groups or individual's incentive to work is necessarily weakened. Of course, this contributes to the wider acceptability of such programs. Since everyone receives a similar benefit, no one can complain that he is working hard but getting no benefit while being taxed to support individuals who are not willing to work but are receiving a benefit. Indeed, that is one of the primary advantages of the nonmeans-tested or universal programs.

Unlike the universal programs, means-tested programs must continually confront this problem of work incentives, both in practical and in political terms. Once a program is directed to those in need, however defined, a "notch problem" inevitably emerges. To help those who are defined as "in need," and yet not help those who are just out of need, creates some basic inequities in the system. It was precisely the concern with these inequities that prompted the very harsh treatment in the nineteenth-century poor laws, whereby the poor person who was dependent upon public charity was to be no better off than the poorest independent worker. Otherwise, it was argued, there was no reason for the independent worker to continue to work.

On the other hand, the dilemma presents itself in a reverse form for those who are defined as being in need and are receiving money from the public dole. Once an individual is on public assistance, there is little economic incentive for him to work. This is especially true because the income from work was, until 1967, taxed at what is now recognized as 100 per cent marginal tax rate. At this rate, any income from work that the individual made was automatically deducted from his public-assistance payments—hardly an incentive to work.

Again, the negative-income-tax proponents were very concerned about building in a work incentive that would both be equitable and solve the "notch problem." Instead of a 100 per cent marginal tax rate, or the 67 per cent marginal tax rate of the current welfare programs,[27] Friedman proposed a marginal tax rate of 50 per cent. Allowing recipients to keep part of their earnings, however, adds to the cost of the program. Friedman solves this problem by providing a basic minimum at a very low level; liberals who want to provide a more generous income floor must face higher cost estimates.

The problem of the incentive to work is certainly a central issue for all but the aged and severely disabled poor. In fact, it is the suspicion on the part of the nonpoor that the poor really do not want to work which results in such demeaning activities of the welfare department as searching for the "man in the house" who is supposed to be working to support the family. Requiring welfare recipients to pick up their checks at the local state employment office is another result of a pervasive belief that welfare recipients prefer to loaf rather than work.

This negative view of welfare recipients has been exacerbated by the rapid growth of Aid to Families with Dependent Children (AFDC), especially in urban areas where the black recipients—although only 43 per cent of the total 1971 caseload—are highly visible. This concern with work incentives is also manifest in the fact that aged public-assistance recipients, for whom this issue is no longer relevant, have higher benefit levels than AFDC families. For example, in Mississippi in 1971 the average monthly payment under Old Age Assistance for an individual was equivalent to the average monthly payment for an entire AFDC family in 1971.[28] If benefit levels are "adequate" for AFDC families, then the fear is that they will refuse to work at the low-paid menial jobs which might be available.

There is more than a little self-interest on the part of the non-poor in their concern for work incentives. They want their low-paid service work done, as illustrated by Senator Long's exclamation with respect to the higher levels of payment for the South in Nixon's Family Assistance Plan (FAP): "I can't get anybody to iron my shirts!"[29] FAP attempted to add a new category—means-tested assistance for working poor families and families with an unemployed father who were not covered by the AFDC Unemployed Parent segment. This plan would have made a great number of men in whole families eligible for assistance, and thus the concern over work incentives became even more pronounced. The introduction of stringent work requirements with the minimum "acceptable" wage set at 75 per cent of the Federal minimum wage or $1.20 an hour was the solution of Wilbur Mills and the House Ways and Means Committee. Even in this form, however, conservative Southern senators were not fully convinced that low-paid jobs in the South would be done. In addition to their concern over work incentives, conservatives were not happy about a program which proposed to put more people on welfare and which would require an additional $3.9 billion of social-welfare expenditures.

For liberal critics, on the other hand, the work requirement was too stringent and the minimum acceptable wage too low. Furthermore, there was little to prevent these requirements from being applied in a demeaning way. Those among the poor most likely to be helped by the program—poor Whites and Blacks in the South—also would be most likely to suffer under the stringent work requirements. At the same time, there would be no protection for public-assistance recipients in the North, where grant levels were already much higher than the minimum program guarantee of $2,400 for a family of four. Liberals who argued for FAP generally did so on the basis that it would establish a "guaranteed minimum income" at least for poor families with children, many of whom currently receive no public-assistance help at all. Some supporters of the negative-income-tax approach were pleased with the adoption of the principle of building this limited floor and the introduction of the marginal tax rate, allowing the poor to keep a portion of their earnings. The proposed marginal tax rate of 67 per cent in FAP II,[30] (the second proposed Family Assistance Plan) only allowed the recipient to keep one-third of his earnings above the first $60 per month. This marginal tax rate is exactly the same as that permitted in the current operation of public assistance, except that in the latter only the first $30 per month is tax-free. Furthermore, a closer examination of the economic incentive to work provided for by the 67 per cent marginal tax rate revealed that this set rate actually understated the effective tax rate since the social-security tax as well as state and local taxes would have to be paid. The effective tax on additional earnings by the poor under FAP, therefore, was much higher than 67 per cent and probably close to 80 per cent. This left little economic incentive to work.

In the fall of 1972, Nixon's Family Assistance Plan (FAP II) failed to pass the Senate for the second time. Nixon himself indicated in February, 1973, that he no longer intends to pursue this particular path toward welfare reform. There is little grief from either liberals or conservatives over the death of this plan. Its defeat, however, has not moved the United States any closer to the goal of greater income equality. FAP, if it had been administered with fairness, would have provided the poor with $3.9 billion more than they are now receiving. True, the plan would have benefited primarily the Southern poor, where the issue of administering the work requirements was problematic. If the money had actually reached those in need in the South, however, it would have radically equalized the distribution of income in a large number of local communities. Richard Armstrong, reporting in *Fortune* magazine, figured out the benefits for one family in the Alabama black belt:

In one of the most dilapidated of the shacks . . . four rooms hammered together from old boards, and patched in spots with cardboard, Mrs. Adie Powell lives with her nine children, her parents, her sister, and her sister's six children. All these nineteen people now manage somehow to survive on $50 a week that Mrs. Powell makes on the assembly line at a local wood-processing plant, the sister's welfare check of $140 a month, and the $192 old-age and social-security pension that Mrs. Powell's parents receive.

Under President Nixon's family-assistance program . . . things would get quite dramatically better for Mrs. Powell and all her kin. As a member of the "working poor" Mrs. Powell could draw $3,552 a year in cash and food stamps to augment her earnings of $2,500 at the mill. Her sister, as an unemployed welfare mother, could draw $3,316 in cash and stamps, and the parents would collect $2,640. Thus, on the effective date of the bill, July 1, 1971, annual household income would almost double overnight from $6,052 to $12,008, the sort of money now enjoyed only by the white merchant and landowner class in Alabama's black belt.[31]

The result would have been a redistribution of income which would have had clear reverberations for the political structure of most of the South in terms of both race and social class.

While rejecting the FAP program, however, Congress did pass the other welfare reforms proposed by President Nixon. The 1972 Amendments to the Social Security Act created a new national assistance program[32] in which the Federal government will take over the administration and at least part of the financing of means-tested assistance to the aged, blind, and disabled. Thus, as of January 1, 1974 the public-assistance programs of Old Age Assistance, Aid to the Blind, and Aid to the Permanently and Totally Disabled will be abolished. A national minimum benefit will be established with full Federal financing, although this minimum is currently exceeded by the actual Old Age Assistance grants in about one-half of the states.[33] Eligibility will be determined by a simple declaration of income, and the program will be administered by the Social Security Administration, which is accustomed to administering benefits as of right. Much of the stigma of these means-tested programs will no doubt be eliminated. This program, then, will do much to improve the status of these recipients for whom the "incentive to work" is not a key issue. Nevertheless, this change effectively isolates the AFDC public-assistance component, leaving mothers and unemployed fathers still subject to the vicissitudes of state and local bureaucracies and public outcries about "welfare chiselers" and loafers. This program, the kingpin of the 1960's welfare crisis, will continue to serve the "undeserving poor," labeled as such because their moral qualities are questioned since they have failed to become economically independent and self-supporting.

CASH TRANSFERS AND THE GOAL OF SOCIAL EQUALITY

The preceding discussion has focused upon different dimensions of various forms of income maintenance programs. The debates over means-testing vs. nonmeans-testing; categorical vs. noncategorical and the related problems of stigma, work incentives, and an adequate income floor have focused upon the consequences of these dimensions for the poor themselves. Although the need for an adequate program of income maintenance is most obvious among this social group, this focus upon the poor tends to obscure the overall question of inequality. While the needs of the poor require that attention be paid to the provision of an adequate income floor without the demeaning aspects of current public assistance programs, a more critical question, in the long run, is the problem of who is to pay for this income floor.

The attempt to build an income floor through the mechanism of social security not only left the floor with many holes, but those who paid for building the floor were not the rich. In fact, individuals whose income derives solely from property ownership may pay not a cent toward the social security checks of the poor. Consequently, the main redistribution of income in the social security program is not from rich to poor, but from those of working age to the retired, from the able to the disabled, from the employed to the unemployed. In addition, when increases in social security benefits are accompanied by increases in the social security tax, it is the working poor who suffer most.

Proposals like the negative income tax and the demogrant, which would provide an income floor for all members of society, quickly run into problems of high costs when the allowances reach levels which would adequately protect a family from poverty. In the negative income tax, high costs can be reduced by increasing the marginal tax rate, but this procedure reduces the economic incentive to work and introduces inequitably high marginal tax rates for those of lowest earning power.

Although proposing a high cost demogrant may well be politically dangerous, the problem of program costs is only insurmountable if it is assumed that the proposed program is to be added on to the Federal budget—with some allowance for the savings from the replacement of public assistance programs—and that these added costs must be paid for through higher taxes. If, instead, a demogrant is combined with radical reform of the tax system itself, then the issue of high costs loses its salience. The McGovern Proposal would have substituted a non-taxable $1,000 per person demogrant for the present system of personal exemptions. The elimination of the personal exemptions, which benefit the poor little or not at all, would have generated more than $60 billion in additional revenue. Furthermore, instead of the present system of progressive rates of taxation on paper and large, gaping loopholes in practice, the McGovern Proposal would have taxed all income without exception at a rate of 33.3 per cent. Overall, the proposed tax reforms would have covered the "costs" of providing the demogrant, in addition to providing revenues sufficient to cover current government operations.[34]

The McGovern Proposal was a loosely worked out plan for income redistribution on the model of what is now called the credit income tax, originally discussed in detail by Rolph.[35] The credit income tax basically provides a mechanism whereby a demogrant becomes workable in practical terms. The mechanism for building a floor of income protection is essentially the same as the negative income tax. Thus, the McGovern proposal, below the breakeven point, is identical to a negative income tax with a minimum guarantee of $4,000 for a family of four, a marginal tax rate of 33.3 per cent, and a breakeven point of about $12,000 where neither benefits are received nor taxes paid.[36] In the credit income tax, however, those above the breakeven point are treated in exactly the same manner as those below. They receive a tax-free demogrant of the same amount as those below the break-even point, which for purposes of simplified administration can be treated as a tax credit; their income is also taxed at the same rate—in this example, 33.3 per cent. It would appear, then, that the credit income tax proposal would be able to eliminate the stigma attached to the receipt of a cash "welfare" grant through the mechanism of treating all members of society in a similar manner.

Moreover, the political appeal of this program would extend beyond those income groups who were receiving direct cash transfers. Indeed, for a family of four which receives all of its income from wages and salaries, the McGovern Proposal would provide tax relief for incomes up to and including $20,000 for 1972. Beyond that income the tax burden would increase, although for those with very high incomes, it would decrease again.[37] This latter problem could be remedied by applying a surtax on incomes of over $50,000. At present, under the current tax law with its many loopholes, even the rich pay an average of only about one-third of their incomes in taxes.

It does appear, then, that there is a technical choice available which would both redistribute income from the rich to the poor and build an adequate floor within the margin of cost acceptable to the vast majority of Americans. While the focus of the credit income tax would be on reducing the inequalities and the distress of the bottom half of the income distribution, other measures, such as a surtax on very high incomes, would be available for reducing inequalities from the top down. The principles of across-the-board equity for the vast majority of Americans would protect those at the bottom from the capricious and demeaning policies which have been so often the lot of the poor receiving public benefits.

Although this choice is available, the redistribution of incomes from the rich to the poor can be resolved only by a moral, rather than a technical choice. If the first priorities of a society are to protect itself from having to pay the way for those whom it deems "too lazy to work" and at the same time, to sustain capitalist privilege in the form of tax loopholes, then no program which both builds an income floor and redistributes income is likely to be enacted. Moreover, if enacted, such a program would soon become riddled with new "loopholes" for the rich and new administrative mechanisms by which the poorest could be made to know the stigma attached to their position. Furthermore, a society which was unconcerned with inequality and distress at the bottom could simply let the value of the demogrant wither away with increasing inflation and affluence. If, on the other hand, the first priority of a society is to protect all of its members from falling far behind in the standards of needs based on the right of each member to not be left out of prosperity, then an income floor and income redistribution as found in the McGovern Proposal would naturally follow.

---

1. Robert J. Lampman, "How Much Does the American System of Transfers Benefit the Poor?," in Leonard H. Goodman, ed., *Economic*

Progress and Social Welfare (New York: Columbia University Press, 1966), Table 4, p. 134.

2. "Report of the Committee on Economic Security," *Economic Security Act*, Hearings before the Committee on Ways and Means (January-February 1935), p. 59.

3. The original act also included the provision for services in maternal and child welfare and public health.

4. Soon after the passage of the Social Security Act, coverage was extended to survivors and later to workers who became permanently and totally disabled.

5. The employer also makes a contribution. However, some argue that this contribution really comes from the employer's wage fund unless the employer can pass on this cost to the consumer in terms of higher prices.

6. Survivors (i.e., primarily widows) who never worked would have earned a benefit as long as their deceased spouse had worked in covered employment.

7. This is due to the fact that the social security tax is levied only up to a specified ceiling and earnings above that ceiling are not taxed.

8. The law permits aid to children "deprived of parental support or care" who are living with their father or other relatives. Until recent changes, the program was primarily directed toward mothers and other female relatives.

9. U.S. Bureau of the Census, *Statistical Abstracts of the United States* (Washington: Government Printing Office, 1972), Table 486, p. 299.

10. See Daniel P. Moynihan, "The Crisis in Welfare," *The Public Interest*, Number 10 (Winter 1968), pp. 3–29. There is no agreement upon the cause of the growth in AFDC. David Gordon's analysis suggests that the primary factor in New York City was the increase in benefit levels which made many more families eligible; see his "Income and Welfare in New York City," *The Public Interest* (Summer 1969), pp. 64–88.

11. These three constituencies reflect, in part, the three emphases of Robert J. Lampman which include the income tax emphasis, the minimum income emphasis and the social fault emphasis; see his "Transfer and Redistribution as a Social Process," in Shirley Jenkins, ed., *Social Security in International Perspective* (New York: Columbia University Press, 1969), pp. 47ff. See also his four conflicting mentalities in *Ends and Means of Reducing Income Poverty* (Chicago: Markham Publishing Co., 1971), pp. 148–49.

12. Alvin L. Schorr, "The Socially Orphaned: The Next Step in Social Security," in his *Explorations in Social Policy* (New York: Basic Books, 1968), pp. 57–68.

13. U.S. Bureau of the Census, *Statistical Abstracts of the United States*, 1972, Table 490, p. 302.

14. Another approach to the integration of the tax system with a system of cash transfers is the credit income tax as outlined by Earl R. Rolph, "A Credit Income Tax," in Theodore Marmor, ed., *Poverty Policy* (New York: Aldine, 1971), pp. 207–17.

15. Milton Friedman, *Capitalism and Freedom* (Chicago: University of Chicago Press, 1962), pp. 190–95.

16. The relation of the minimum guarantee, the marginal tax rate, and the break-even point where no further benefits are obtained is represented by the formula:

$$\text{marginal tax rate} = \frac{\text{minimum guarantee}}{\text{break-even point}}$$

17. It should be noted that people work for reasons other than economic gain.

18. The negative-income-tax plans of Tobin and Lampman are discussed in George Hildebrand, *Poverty, Income Maintenance, and the Negative Income Tax* (Ithaca: New York State School of Industrial and Labor Relations, Cornell University, 1967), Chapters V and VI.

19. See Daniel P. Moynihan, "Annals of Politics," in *The New Yorker* (January 27, 1973), pp. 57ff.

20. Office of Economic Opportunity, *The Poor in 1970: A Chart Book*, Chart 15, p. 36.

21. Only 23 states implemented the program. See Joel F. Handler, *Reforming the Poor* (New York: Basic Books, 1972), p. 74.

22. Lampman, "How Much Does the American System of Transfers Benefit the Poor?," Table 5, p. 136.

23. *Ibid.*

24. *The New York Times* (May 26, 1972), p. 42.

25. This concept of efficiency overlooks, however, the expense of the large welfare bureaucracy required to implement the means test, estimated to be about $1.4 billion in 1972.

26. Lampman, *op. cit.*, Table 5, p. 136.

27. Since 1967, welfare recipients are permitted to keep the first $30 of earnings each month after which they only keep one-third of each additional dollar earned, so they now have a marginal tax rate of 67 per cent.

28. U.S. Bureau of the Census, *Statistical Abstracts of the United States,* 1972, Table 491, p. 302.

29. Reported in James Welsh, "Welfare Reform: born, Aug. 8, 1969, died, Oct. 4, 1972," in *The New York Times Magazine* (January 7, 1973), p. 16.

30. This refers to the second version of the Family Assistance Plan. In the original version the tax rate was 50 per cent. See Handler, p. 100, for further details.

31. As quoted in Daniel P. Moynihan, "Annals of Politics," *The New Yorker* (January 27, 1973), p. 67.

32. See Robert M. Ball, "Social Security Amendments of 1972: Summary and Legislative History," *Social Security Bulletin* (March 1973), pp. 23–5.

33. States may supplement benefits up to current levels. The Federal

minimum grant is expected to include a sufficient allowance for food so that beneficiaries will no longer be eligible for food programs.

34. For details and analysis of the McGovern Proposal see his article "How the Economy Should Be Changed," *The New York Review of Books* (May 4, 1972), pp. 7–11, and Russell Lidman, "Cost and Distributional Implications of McGovern's Minimum Income Grant Proposal," Discussion Paper 131–72 (Madison, Wisconsin: University of Wisconsin, Institute for Research on Poverty, June, 1972).

35. Rolph, "A Credit Income Tax," pp. 207–17. For another version see Lee Rainwater, "Economic Inequality and the Credit Income Tax," *Working Papers for a New Society*, 1 (Spring 1973), pp. 56–60.

36. Everyone would calculate his tax with exactly the same formula; using this example:

Net tax liability = (33.3 per cent of income) − $1,000 for each family member. If the net tax liability was negative then the family would receive a cash grant for the amount, if positive the family would pay that amount in taxes. For a family of four with an income of $12,012 the net tax would be (33.3 per cent of $12,012) − $4,000 or zero.

37. These estimates are made by Lidman, *op. cit.*, Table 10, p. 26.

9
An End to Inequality?

Sally Bould Van Til
Jon Van Til

The debate over antipoverty programs and policies in the 1960's focused on two major questions: Why are people poor and what can be done to lift poor people out of poverty? In seeking answers to both questions, the focus was typically directed toward the poor themselves. Thus, one group of social scientists came to discuss poverty and derive strategies to reduce it in terms of the "culture of poverty," a position often used to explain poverty in terms of the characteristics of poor persons themselves. As one text explains it:

> Although virtually all sociologists agree that the behaviors of different classes have both cultural and situational sources, there is considerable disagreement on the relative importance of the two. Many emphasize the cultural sources and speak of "social class subcultures" or of a "culture of poverty." The latter is believed to be a way of life guided by values transmitted from one generation to another, a collective adaptation of the poor to their adverse conditions. . . . Other observers believe that the behaviors attributed to the culture of poverty are actually individual responses to the conditions of economic deprivation and social dishonor. According to this point of view, the values of the poor are basically the same as those of higher strata; however, because of situational restrictions, they do not result in the same overt behaviors.[1]

Not all social scientists and policy makers subscribe to the "culture-of-poverty" position; the second major explanation adopted was that of the "situational" or "blocked-opportunity" position. The same source quoted above notes that:

If the situational view is correct, once the social environment of the poor is changed, their behavior will quickly come to resemble that of the solid middle classes. . . . If, however, there is a culture of poverty, many of the poor will not respond readily or at all to increased opportunities or other situational changes. Rather, the values of the poor that are maladaptive in the long run will have to be extinguished, or the society's guardians will have to accept the fact that American middle-class values are perhaps, after all, not the highest point of moral evolution, that other values may be equally suitable to those who hold them.[2]

The policy implication of the culture-of-poverty hypothesis is that the poor must be resocialized to accept mainstream or middle-class values. Such resocialization, it was thought by the adherents of this position, would result in a stronger attachment toward work and achievement in the economic order, and, therefore, in a higher income for poor persons. The blocked-opportunity position, on the other hand, placed greater emphasis upon the economic life chances available to the poor. Those social programs of the 1960's that were based on this hypothesis sought to enable the poor to compete more effectively in the economic structure through the provision of better educational opportunities and job training. In the last analysis, however, the blocked-opportunity approach of the 1960's was not that different from the culture-of-poverty approach. In the policies to which they gave rise, both approaches focused almost exclusively upon the poor themselves, seeking to change their competitive advantage either through the inculcation of middle-class values or by more direct measures aimed at making them better able to compete for jobs in the labor market.

An obvious flaw in the design of the antipoverty programs of the 1960's may thus be identified: Neither of the two basic approaches offered much help to those poor persons who could not be expected to support themselves in the labor market. Thus, the aged, the disabled, and children, as well as mothers who were the sole support of small children, could not be lifted out of poverty through such programs as job training. It was this realization of the limits of this service strategy which, in part, led to the Federal government's reassessment of income-maintenance programs. Nevertheless, the proposals of the President's Commission on Income Maintenance Programs and the Nixon Family Assistance Plan continued to focus exclusively upon the poor, and upon narrow conceptions of poverty reduction. The question of the overall degree of inequality has been largely ignored by official policy makers.

The assumption that poverty can be reduced or eliminated without simultaneously attending to the reduction of overall inequality in society is increasingly being challenged by social scientists.[3] Much recent evidence points to the fact that the poor are not isolated from the operation of the rest of society. Attitude studies among the poor show that the majority are *not* trapped in a culture of poverty, but instead do have high aspirations toward achieving a comfortable level of living and are willing to work in order to achieve those aspirations. One large-scale recent study of the welfare poor concludes:

> Evidence from this study unambiguously supports the following conclusion: Poor people—males and females, Blacks and Whites, youths and adults—identify their self-esteem with work as strongly as do the nonpoor. They express as much willingness to take job training if unable to earn a living and to work, even if they were to have an adequate income. They have, moreover, as high life aspirations as do the nonpoor, and want the same things, among them a good education and a nice place to live. This study reveals no differences between poor and nonpoor when it comes to life goals and wanting to work.[4]

The problem is not that most of the poor are isolated from the economic sphere of society. They do, indeed, have opportunities for work in most cases. The kinds of jobs that the poor most often have —casual, irregular jobs and low-wage jobs—fit them into the economic structure in such a way that the economic system functions more smoothly. In many ways, then, the poor *are* integrated into the rest of society, and by their marginal position they perform certain important functions for that society. Any program that truly eliminates poverty, it follows, implies basic changes in the structure of society itself. Poverty, in other words, serves several important functions for the maintenance of our economic system; some are poor and, as a consequence, others are better off.

An important function served by poor people, first identified by Marx, is their supplying a "reserve army of the unemployed." While modern capitalist states have taken measures to counteract the "boom and bust" which was inherent in early capitalism, it is now recognized that a capitalist system cannot operate at a permanent level of full employment, since full employment results in a level of inflation which the majority in the society are unwilling to tolerate. The "trade-off" between inflation and unemployment, as indicated in Chapter 7, means that once inflation becomes a serious problem for the majority in society, the level of unemployment is allowed to rise. It is the poor who pay the highest price—because they are most likely to be laid off—and the rest of society benefits through lower rates of inflation. Since the poor have little political power, they can be forced to absorb the social costs involved in reducing the rate of inflation.[5]

When unemployment gets out of hand, however, the poor are likely to be disruptive, so that specific institutions, notably public welfare, are designed to mollify such disruptive tendencies and give the poor some money to tide them over periods of excessively high unemployment. But, in the long run, the push is always to get the poor back to work, even at very low-paying jobs, and to force them off welfare into workfare, a major concern of the current Nixon Administration. The effort to reduce the welfare rolls that has become so dominant a political theme in the 1970's follows a decade of rapid expansion of the rolls, a decade in which the poor manifested the credibility of disruption by both active social movements and civil disorder. The process tends to be cyclical: When the movement is exhausted and the threat of disruption reduced, the majority nonpoor turns to the task of weeding out the welfare rolls.[6]

A similar cycle of welfare is often used in conjunction with seasonal jobs. In the South, welfare payments tend to be made in winter when agricultural work is scarce. During the summer season workers are needed for low-paid farm jobs and, coincidentally, the welfare rolls are cut.

The poor also provide benefits for the majority in society because they can be forced to accept jobs which pay very low wages. Such low-wage jobs permit the prices of goods and services thereby produced to be lower than they would be if such jobs paid adequate wages.[7] This phenomenon is particularly prevalent in the area of service, where wages are notoriously low for services like laundry, parking, child care, and household help. The middle class has come to expect these services to be provided at low wages, and the concept of a "living wage" has not been applied to such occupations. The result is a gain in real income for the nonpoor, especially for the middle and upper classes, who are the major purchasers of these services.

A third way in which the poor are useful to the majority nonpoor in American society is noted by Herbert Gans in a fascinating article on "The Positive Functions of Poverty":

> The poor, being powerless, can be made to absorb the economic and political costs of change and growth in American society. During the 19th

century they did the backbreaking work that built the cities; today they are pushed out of their neighborhoods to make room for "progress." Urban renewal projects to hold middle class taxpayers and stores in the city, and expressways to enable suburbanites to commute downtown have typically been located in poor neighborhoods, since no other group will allow itself to be displaced. For much the same reason, urban universities, hospitals, and civic centers also expand into land occupied by the poor. The major costs of the industrialization of agriculture in America have been borne by the poor, who are pushed off the land without recompense, just as in earlier centuries in Europe, they bore the brunt of the transformations of agrarian societies into industrial ones. The poor have also paid a large share of the human cost of the growth of American power overseas, for they have provided many of the footsoldiers for Vietnam and other wars.[8]

The powerlessness of the poor is also reflected in lower rates of voter registration and voting. These rates are particularly important in allowing middle- and working-class interests to persist in the control of many mayoralties in American cities, despite the fact that poor persons comprise a large proportion of the population in most of these cities.

Any change in the current conditions of poverty in American society would leave the nonpoor less well off than they currently are. Daniel P. Moynihan, an adviser to two Presidents on urban affairs, recognizes this important function of poverty and its integral relationship to the overall system of stratification. Addressing himself to a group of "comfortable and affluent political liberals," he first clarifies for his listeners their place in the system of stratification: Each of them is "a person who has shared considerably in the rewards of American life and can look forward to a continued sharing and if anything, on more favorable terms." But such benefits could not continue if poverty were, in fact, to be eliminated and a more equal society created:

There are doubtless those among us so ungrateful or so idealistic as to wish or be willing to give it all up in favor of a regime not yet more generous in its distribution of worldly and psychic goods, but there is none of us, I repeat, who would not in fact have something considerable of both of these to lose in the exchange.[9]

Moynihan indicates, moreover, that more than just money is at stake; a more equal society would also mean a loss of relative status for those who are currently benefiting from existing inequalities. The stereotype of the poor as shiftless and lazy serves another function: that is to affirm the value of hard work and thereby to justify the unequal distribution of material rewards. Those who benefit from the system, the middle and upper classes, can view their material benefits as a reflection of their inherent worth.

Like crime, then, poverty, with its disreputable connotation, may be seen as "bound up with the fundamental conditions of social life," and, in capitalist societies, is "indispensable to the normal evolution of morality and law." [10] In the mid-twentieth century, poverty is no longer a crime; neither is the poor individual viewed as morally depraved. It is, rather, their "whole way of life"—a life that stresses immediate gratification—which is now held responsible for the plight of the poor. And this way of life is the mirror image of the cultural ideal. The virtues of the thrifty, frugal, hard-working individual who plans carefully for the future are upheld by his perception of the improvidence and laziness of the poor. As long as this cultural ideal persists,[11] its reflection in the mirror will remain.

In contrast to the condemnation of the "whole way of life" of the poor in the culture-of-poverty model, the blocked-opportunity model suggests a more activist, humane, and liberal set of policies. This latter view of the poor, although not as popular as the cultural view,[12] stresses the important American value of "equality of opportunity." A sense of fairness among many Americans is offended when some persons are denied equal opportunity on the basis of race or social background. The goal of achieving equality of opportunity, however, does not include the achievement of equality of results.

Blocked-opportunity theorists stress that the poor do have values and aspirations like the rest of us, but differ only in the absence of economic opportunities available to them. The poor are seen to resemble the middle class in that they respond to available opportunities. They differ from the middle class in that they have few such opportunities available to them upon which to capitalize. The focus is more upon the inadequacies of opportunity structures in the society at large than upon the inadequacies of poor persons, although policies implemented under this model in the 1960's generally emphasized manipulating the characteristics of poor persons rather than manipulating the system. Under this model the poor, too, should be adequately equipped for the climb up the opportunity ladder. Policy planners under this model, then, argue for more and better education and job training, an end to discrimination, and, in some cases, the provision of more jobs. Many also suggest that a minimum income standard must be assured so that the first step may be secured on the opportunity ladder.

The blocked-opportunity model, like the culture-of-poverty model, however, tends to ignore the important gains that accrue to the nonpoor from poverty and inequality. Improving education and job-related skills of poor persons does not reduce the level of unemployment in society, nor does it reduce the number of low-wage jobs. Furthermore, as we argued in Chapter 2, reducing the amount of educational inequality does not lead to an automatic reduction in income inequality. If everyone were to achieve at least a high-school education, for example, that would probably not significantly affect the distribution of inequality. Inequality of incomes, as Jencks shows, is built into our economic structure. As long as there are large numbers of low-wage jobs that need to be filled, the pressure will be put upon those at the bottom of the stratification system to fill those jobs. This pressure results from the majority's desire to have such jobs performed at low wages. Senator Long's concern about getting someone to iron his shirts, after welfare reform, is not simply one of getting the job done, but of getting it done cheaply. If he were willing to pay five dollars an hour to have his shirts ironed, there would be no question that the Senator could get the job done.

On careful analysis, it may be seen that the policies flowing from both the culture-of-poverty theory and the blocked-opportunity model rest upon the assumption that it is sufficient to assure equality of opportunity in society. The debate between the two positions often boils down to arguing which should come first—the creation of opportunities or the resocialization of the poor.[13] But a model of equality of opportunity fails to confront the basic nature of the stratification system itself. Indeed, the sociological model of stratification in modern industrial society developed by Davis and Moore,[14] which was identified in Chapter 1 as the consensus theory of stratification, is legitimated on the basis of equality of opportunity and a corresponding emphasis upon the value of achievement in order to induce qualified individuals to fulfill functionally important positions. Even if the role of the family in the inheritance of privilege could be eliminated, the institutionalized inequality of rewards would remain. Ironing shirts would still command a poverty wage, even if all individuals had an equal chance of ending up in such a low-wage job.

In addition, full equality of opportunity would not eliminate differences in mental and physical capacities, as is so clearly argued in Michael Young's fantasy on the rise of the meritocracy.[15] In

Young's novel, British society is portrayed as seeking to provide perfect equality of opportunity so that the fittest persons rise to the top. The end result would be to produce a society as inegalitarian as the one that exists at the present time; those at the bottom, however, would have the added burden of having their "unfitness" confirmed by the social system. Indeed, if all but genetic differences were eliminated, there would be ample room for the creation of a new underclass. Research on differences in achievement on I.Q. tests, as biased as these tests are, shows that the genetic component plays an important role in explaining from 40 to 60 per cent of the variance.[16]

Nevertheless, according to the research of Bowles and Gintis, American society is in no danger of creating a meritocracy. Once the social-class-background factor is controlled, I.Q. contributes very little in explaining economic success or failure. Additionally they point out that:

. . . the fact that economic success tends to run in the family arises almost completely independently from any genetic inheritance of I.Q. . . . A family's position in the class structure is reproduced primarily by mechanisms operating independently of the inheritance, production, and certification of intellectual skills.[17]

In view of the evidence that a "meritocracy" does not exist, Bowles and Gintis suggest that the popular belief in it does serve an important function in the legitimation of inequalities within existing economic structures. This legitimation applies with a vengeance to the economic failures of our society. Over half of a sample of the adult population cited as "very important" reasons for poverty the "lack of thrift and proper money management by poor people," "lack of effort by the poor themselves," and "lack of ability and talent among poor people."[18] Even without full equality of opportunity this achievement ethic is used to justify the present treatment of the poor as marginal misfits. It is the ideology of the "open class" system which, on the one hand, provides for the socialization of the poor into mainstream aspirations while, on the other hand, it is used to justify their unequal treatment by mainstream institutions. In that form, equality of opportunity is simply a hoax on the poor, a dirty trick that is played upon them by persons intent on keeping them at the bottom.

Where equality of opportunity does not exist, much of the behavior of the poor which is now attributed to their being trapped in a culture of poverty might be better understood in terms of their being trapped at the bottom of a statification system which views poverty as a sign of personal failing. Under such a system, the poor have little choice but to develop survival techniques which serve as safety valves to promote limited feelings of self-respect and self-worth. Nevertheless, the poor are roundly condemned for their use of such survival techniques as female-based households and the use of public welfare. Over two-thirds of a sample of American adults agreed with the statement that "many people getting welfare are not honest about their need." [19]

The poor, owing to their position in the stratification system, appear better able to perceive the structure of privilege in society for what it is, not as simply "the natural order of things" or an inevitable consequence of economic structure. The poor, and especially the Black poor, tend to view social institutions as providing unequal treatment for themselves and the more affluent and see themselves as having the least power and influence in government.[20] Furthermore, the poor are least likely to view people on relief as lazy[21] and to believe that unemployment is the individual's own fault.[22] The view from the bottom is apparently less clouded with the ideology of "classlessness" and "opportunity" than that from the higher sectors of society. The mainstream social institutions—political, economic, educational, and welfare—present constant reminders to the poor that others in society are provided for better. Bureaucracies are not impartial; if they were, the poor would suffer only as much as the rest of us. Even those institutions which are designed specifically to serve the poor, such as departments of public assistance, often operate on subjective principles of justice.[23] These institutions frequently distinguish between the deserving and the undeserving poor and personal characteristics often determine this judgment. The undeserving are those who are either unable or unwilling to project a belief in mainstream values.

The perceptions of the poor are, on the whole, accurate: they *are* the primary victims of social inequality. Not only are they denied sustenance and opportunity, but they are kept at the bottom by the workings of major social institutions. In the marketplace, they are seen as unable to contribute sufficient "net marginal productivity" to make their labor worth buying at a decent wage. Thus, they often become dependent upon cash assistance, usually in the form of welfare. Nevertheless, increasing the level of welfare payments does not substantially alter the behavior of the poor. Even though these increased payments provide a subsistence income, they do not affect the basic conditions of life at the bottom. The poor still pay more for what they get; the housing market and the job market remain the same. The schools to which they send their children have not changed; their access to good health care is as poor as always. They still face the capriciousness of the welfare department, manipulated by reactionary state legislators. Furthermore, they have little power to effect any changes in these circumstances.

What does all this mean for the social change that may be required to assure an end to social inequality? First, reducing income inequality, though an important step toward full equality, is not sufficient as a means. Equality must also be advanced simultaneously in its other dimensions, including wealth, education, power, and occupational status. Social change toward the achievement of equality must be multidimensional, for inequality itself is multidimensional. The poor have learned, through bitter experience, to perceive privilege; the elimination of privilege on one dimension is not likely to blind them to its persistence on other dimensions. They will reserve their commitment to mainstream values and preserve their own "designs for living" until the larger society provides not only equality of opportunity, but also equality of results.

The phrase "equality of results," or "full equality," suggests several ideas that have not been widely accepted in the American experience. Traditionally, we have been satisfied to choose "equality of opportunity" as a goal, and to assume that it is right and just that vast inequalities of income be allowed to result as long as the race is fairly run from an even start. Of course, we have never been able to achieve the fair and even start imagined by those who talk about equal opportunity. The inheritance of wealth advantages some over others; enriched family backgrounds give a quickened step to those fortunate enough to "choose" the proper parents.

But even with equality of opportunity, inequality would persist —a function of luck, skill, socialization, effort, and heredity. Thus, the question remains: How much equality can we expect to achieve within the context of an achievement-oriented, late capitalist economic system? Heilbroner argues that while the elimination of capitalist privilege[24] is not possible, the elimination of poverty is; a greater equality could be achieved among the masses, while preserving the perquisites of the elite.

For the sake of brevity, we will examine the possibility of achieving equality among the masses while preserving the privilege of elites in the case of income equalization only. Income equalization is seen as a necessary, although not sufficient, condition for the elimination of poverty. A policy of radical income equalization implies 1) a redistribution of income to provide for those who do not have access to the market economy (e.g., the aged, sick, and disabled), and 2) an equalization of wages for those who are participating in the labor force.[25] Heilbroner implies that these two factors are independent of capitalist privilege.

We would question this conclusion on the first point by examining the Swedish experience, certainly farther along the road to an egalitarian society than the United States. What has occurred in Sweden's effort to resdistribute income is a "ceiling" effect. The original distribution of income places a limitation upon the extent to which equality can be achieved by later redistributing it such that this distribution of income, even in Sweden, is directly related to capitalist privilege.

Similarly, there appears to be a limitation on the achievement of wage equalization as long as corporate power and privilege remain. Low wages are not so much the result of capitalist exploitation as they are a reflection of inequality of power and privilege within the corporate world. Certain industries, which are now identified as the "low-wage industries," with high levels of competition and low profit margins, cannot afford to pay more than poverty wages even in boom times. Furthermore, they do not benefit from government measures to aid business, measures which generally serve the large corporations, which can thus afford to pay high wages.[26]

Neither is planning the panacea for the problem of provision of jobs for all those who want them. Even the planned societies of Western Europe are experiencing rising unemployment rates and are beginning to accept them as "trade-offs" for lower rates of inflation. The United States, meanwhile, is evolving to a new definition of full employment—4.5 per cent unemployment—and some predict that this definition will be further escalated.[27] Even if all jobs paid adequate wages, the instability of employment would create the familiar group of "last hired, first fired."

It is thus difficult to perceive how poverty could be eliminated without at the same time eliminating capitalist privilege. Like the ideology of "equality of opportunity," capitalist privilege creates the conditions for the persistence of a marginal minority underclass whose low economic position will be reinforced by low status and low power. In the short run, however, government policies could be established for the creation of a more equal distribution of income and wealth by means of a tax reform together with a guaranteed annual income at a level above mere subsistence. Such tax reforms should at least eliminate the "tax welfare" payments totaling over two billion dollars which are now received by the three thousand families who have yearly incomes in excess of one million dollars.[28] Of course, these lucrative tax loopholes for the wealthy are an important aspect of capitalist privilege in the American political economy.

Let us assume that the above policies are possible—and they are possible, we believe, only under the conditions described by Gans: that we all, rich and poor, suffer from the current "American malaise" in a "conflict-ridden society." [29] Thus, the rich and the not-so-rich may be willing to make some sacrifices—especially if the model is individualistic—in return for the better society that these measures of increasing income equality promise. But what of that promise? The no-longer-poor will not lose their perception of privilege overnight. Families receiving the Welfare Rights Organization's suggested guaranteed annual income of $6,500 will still be living in a society where the president of a bankrupt railroad could receive an after-tax income of over $100,000. And the institutions which have abused them for so long would, perhaps, raise their level of service to that of the hardly elevated level already received by the current middle class.

Given these conditions, the ex-poor are less likely to emerge "content," and are more likely to experience the revolution of rising expectations. Their dissatisfactions will no doubt be echoed by many others. The result of all this is that social conflict is not likely to cease—it may even increase. Those who sacrificed some of their privilege to raise the incomes of the poor in return for a better— read "more peaceful"—society, will no doubt feel cheated and demand that the movement toward equality be stopped, if not repealed altogether. We will hear much more in such times of the "limits of social policy." [30]

What, then, are the possible futures of inequality and privilege in America? First, Americans may seek to retrench behind the traditional structures and values of capitalism—rewarding the wealthy, the plucky, and the lucky—while retarding the human development of those upon whom the doors of opportunity have closed. This choice will surely mean the persistence and intensification of discontent, the continuing rise of crime and social disorganization, and, ultimately, so severe a test of our democratic institutions that the country may be driven to the fascistic control of all social institutions by the most powerful economic combines and their political puppets.

A second possible future is the emergence of a radically egalitarian social order from a violent revolution. The experience of the 1960's had led many to believe in this possibility in the near future. That vision, however, appears to have receded farther into the future; in the 1970's social protests have become more personal than political.

Does the threat of repression on the one hand, and the improbability of revolution on the other, mean that there must be no immediate future for the principles of equality? Certainly, capitalist privilege presents an enormous stumbling block to any development of values which place first priority upon the idea that all human beings deserve an equal chance for personal development and sustenance. Nevertheless, there are numerous signs in the offing that capitalism's adaptive capacity may be weakening, thereby permitting new ideas to enter into the cracks of the old system.

Although McGovern's Proposal for a modified demogrant combined with tax reform proved to be abortive in the 1972 Presidential campaign, the concept of a more equitable distribution of income has a powerful potential political impact. First, survey results show that public opinion classifies the "rich" as those who have incomes of 125 per cent more than an income necessary to "get along" and only twice as much as a "comfortable" income.[31] Such income differentials represent a radical equalization by present standards. Second, and perhaps even more important, the redistribution of income and wealth would have a very practical appeal; many millions of Americans, indeed a clear majority of us, would benefit from a plan of income distribution that assured each adult a yearly income of at least $1,500 in the form of a credit income tax like the one outlined by Rainwater.[32] Such a plan would directly benefit a majority of Americans, and would not interfere with a work incentive that provides somewhat higher pay for more important jobs.

With such a change in our income structure, surprisingly few changes should be expected in work effort. Many people work for more than the income involved—for their self-esteem, identity, and interest in changing aspects of the world. Survey results indicate that 80 per cent of respondents report that they would continue to work even if they had enough money to live comfortably without working.[33] This desire to work is as strong among the hard-core unemployed as it is among blue-collar and white-collar workers.[34]

In the long run, reducing the importance of the economic incentive may serve to promote changes which emphasize other motivations to work. Even now the economic incentive is wearing thin for assembly-line workers, who are becoming increasingly discontented with their alienating work and are demanding more humane, if not more creative, working conditions. The belief that power hierarchies and wage differentiation must be maintained in the work place for efficient production will be increasingly challenged by the resistance of those at the bottom of the hierarchy who, in fact, produce. The specter of "economic collapse" is probably a much more real possibility under the current organization of production than it would be if economic conditions and power relations on the job were equalized.

While the odds for change in the distribution of wealth and income may appear long, such change is far from impossible, and may even become necessary. The achievement of greater equality in American society, however, will involve not just political struggle, but *continuing* political struggle. Herbert Gans has written that "equality is likely to become an increasingly insistent item on the agenda of American politics."[35] We hope that he is correct, although neither the process nor the outcome is certain.

1. Richard L. Roe, publisher, social sciences, *Society Today* (Delmar, California: CRM Books, 1971), p. 228.

2. *Ibid.*, p. 230.

3. See Herbert J. Gans, "The New Egalitarianism," *Saturday Review*, LV (May 6, 1972), pp. 43–46; and S. M. Miller and Pamela Roby, *The Future of Inequality* (New York: Basic Books, 1970).

4. Leonard Goodwin, *Do the Poor Want to Work?* (Washington, D.C.: The Brookings Institution, 1972), p. 112.

5. James Tobin, in "Inflation and Unemployment," *American Economic Review* (March 1971), suggests that the social costs of inflation have been overemphasized (pp. 15–17).

6. See Francis Fox Piven and Richard A. Cloward, *Regulating the Poor* (New York: Pantheon Books, 1971).

7. Howard Wachtel, "Capitalism and Poverty in America: Paradox or Contradiction?," *American Economic Review* (May 1972), p. 188.

8. Herbert J. Gans, "The Positive Functions of Poverty," *American Journal of Sociology*, 78 (September 1972), pp. 275–89.

9. Daniel P. Moynihan, quoted in Charles A. Valentine, *Culture and Poverty* (Chicago: University of Chicago Press, 1968), p. 41.

10. Emile Durkheim, *The Rules of Sociological Method* (Glencoe, Ill.: The Free Press of Glencoe, 1950), p. 70.

11. This cultural ideal is closely tied in with the development of capitalism so that it is not surprising that Oscar Lewis finds a culture of poverty to be characteristic of capitalist societies but not of socialist ones. See Oscar Lewis, "The Culture of Poverty," in Daniel P. Moynihan, ed., *On Understanding Poverty* (New York: Basic Books, 1968), pp. 194–99.

12. Only about one-third of adult Americans indicate that "failure of society to provide good schools" and "prejudice and discrimination against Negroes" were very important causes of poverty. See Joe R. Feagin, "Poverty: We Still Believe God Helps Those Who Help Themselves," *Psychology Today*, 6 (November 1972), p. 104.

13. Alvin D. Zalinger, "Job Training Programs: Motivational and Structural Dimensions" in *Poverty and Human Resources Abstracts*, 4 (May–June 1969), pp. 5–13.

14. Kingsley Davis and Wilbert E. Moore, "On Principles of Stratification," *American Sociological Review*, 10 (April 1945), pp. 242–49.

15. Michael Young, *The Rise of the Meritocracy, 1970–2033* (Baltimore: Penguin Books, 1961).

16. Jencks et al., *Inequality*, pp. 266–319.

17. Samuel Bowles and Herbert Gintis, "I.Q. in the U.S. Class Structure," *Social Policy* (January–February 1973), p. 71.

18. Feagin, "Poverty: We Still Believe God Helps Those Who Help Themselves," p. 104.

19. *Ibid.*, p. 107.

20. William H. Form and Joan Huber, "Income, Race and the Ideology of Political Efficacy" (Urbana: Institute of Labor and Industrial Relations of the University of Illinois, Reprint 221, 1971).

21. *Ibid.*

22. Robert W. Miller, Frederick A. Zeller, and Harry R. Blaine, "Implications of Social Class Differences in Beliefs Concerning Causes of Unemployment" (Morgantown: Office of Research and Development, West Virginia University Research Series 2, 1968).

23. David Matza, *Delinquency and Drift* (New York: John Wiley and Sons, 1964). Matza calls this subjective decision making "kadi justice."

24. Heilbroner identified the core institutions of privilege in capitalism as "the right to earn private benefit from the use of the means of production and the right to utilize the dynamic forces of the market place for private enrichment." Robert L. Heilbroner, *The Limits of American Capitalism* (New York: Harper and Row, 1965), p. 71. This results in a structure of wealth and income which, we would add, is preserved through the right of inheritance.

25. In order to simplify the argument here, those few individuals with very high incomes from investments are ignored for the moment.

26. Barry Bluestone, "Economic Theory and the Fate of the Poor," *Social Policy*, 2 (January–February 1972), pp. 30ff.

27. Melville Ulmer, "Things You Never Knew About Unemployment," *The New Republic,* 166 (May 6, 1972), p. 14.

28. Philip Stern, *The Rape of the Taxpayer* (New York: Random House, 1973), defines "tax welfare" payments as the benefits of tax forgiveness to those who qualify for exemptions, deductions, and loopholes. The result is the same as welfare payments—the individual benefiting from "tax welfare" payments is richer by that amount, and the U.S. Government is poorer. See pp. 8–9.

29. Herbert J. Gans, "The New Egalitarianism," p. 46.

30. Nathan Glazer, "The Limits of Social Policy," *Commentary,* 52 (September 1972), pp. 51–58.

31. Lee Rainwater, "Economic Inequality and the Credit Income Tax," *Working Papers for a New Society,* 1 (Spring 1973), p. 53.

32. *Ibid.,* pp. 56–59.

33. Nancy C. Morse and Robert S. Weiss, "The Function and Meaning of Work and the Job," *American Sociological Review,* 20 (April 1955), Table I, p. 192.

34. See Roy H. Kaplan and Curt Tausky, "Work and the Welfare Cadillac: The Function of and Commitment to Work Among the Hard-Core Unemployed," *Social Problems,* 19 (Spring 1972), Table 5, p. 479.

35. Herbert Gans, "The New Egalitarianism," p. 46.

Annotated Bibliography

Our goals here are three: To highlight comparatively recent and remarkable publications, to stress those available in inexpensive paperback editions, and to represent a fairly wide range of relevant material. We have deliberately excluded reference to books cited often in the main body of this book, and "classics" widely known in the field, out of deference to our tight space limitations. We mean this only as a "sampler," and welcome your nominations for inclusion in revised later editions of this bibliography.

Bernello, C. George and Roussopoulos, Dimitrios, eds. *The Case for Participatory Democracy: Some Prospects for a Radical Society*. New York: Viking, 1971.

Twenty-one essays whose authors "seek for structural changes in a system that is closing out true democracy and that is robbing people of a chance to have politically meaningful identities within their culture. . . . It is in the serious consideration of alternative modes of social organization that our social and political theory is weakest, and, we hope, it is here that the real contribution of this collection lies."

Bookchin, Murray. *Post-Scarcity Anarchism*. New York: Ramparts Press, 1971.

". . . It is the closest thing I've seen to a vision both practical and transcendent. Anyone who wants to make revolution in this country should read it and reckon with it. . . ." Todd Gitlin, *The Nation* (March 6, 1972), p. 309.

Coser, Rose Laub. *Life Cycle and Achievement in America*. New York: Harper Torchbooks, 1969.

"It is because of the salience of occupational roles for the individual self-image as well as for the value climate of our social institutions that the (nine) papers in this volume have been so selected as to show the relevance of structural features—class positions and role relationships—for the various stages of socialization during the life cycle."

Domhoff, G. William. *The Higher Circles: The Governing Class in America*. New York: Vintage, 1971.

Includes chapters on how the Power Elite make foreign policy, shape social legislation, and co-join with the CIA in a struggle for our minds.

Closes with essays that defend this view by contrasting it with those of pluralists and ultraconservatives.

Domhoff, G. William. *Who Rules America?* Englewood Cliffs: Prentice-Hall (Spectrum Books), 1967.

An attempt to ground Mills' "power elite" in Baltzell's "American business aristocracy" and Sweezy's "ruling class," and to show that Dahl's finding of "pluralism" on the local level is not incompatible with the idea of a national upper class that is also a governing class.

Farber, Jerry. *The University of Tomorrowland.* New York: Pocket Books, 1972.

Nine essays, including "Why People Love Capitalism," a singular effort to get at the root sources of our support of a system condemned as "institutionalized selfishness, institutionalized blindness, institutionalized theft."

Feldman, Saul D., and Thielbar, G. W. *Life Styles: Diversity in American Society.*

Includes thirty-six essays covering sex roles and life-styles, ethnic life-styles, geographic dimensions of life-styles, and others.

Fischer, George, ed. *The Revival of American Socialism. Selected Papers of the Socialist Scholars Conference.* New York: Oxford University Press, 1971.

"In the 1960's, the United States experienced a swift rise of both rejection of the status quo and its defense by repression. The same decade gave birth to broad movements for social change, and with it began a revival of American socialism. The story of how that revival started is told in part" in this work.

Gordon, David M. *Theories of Poverty and Underemployment.* Lexington, Mass.: D. C. Heath, 1972.

Winner of the 1973 C. Wright Mills Award as the best book on a contemporary social problem. The author skillfully applies the tools of radical economics to the study of inequality.

Grey, Alan L. *Class and Personality in Society.* New York: Atherton Press, 1969.

Eight essays that explore the uses of psychoanalytically based theory in social-class analysis.

Handler, Joel F. *Reforming the Poor.* New York: Basic Books, 1972.

A detailed exploration of major avenues of welfare reform, with descriptions of programs and analyses of their prospects for adoption.

Harrington, Michael. *Toward a Democratic Left: A Radical Program for a New Majority.* New York: Penguin, 1969.

A major account of a reform program and movement which socialists and radicals can—and must—support, but which appeals to the most traditional American aspirations for reform as well.

Howe, Irving, ed. *The World of the Blue Collar Worker*. New York: Quadrangle Press, 1972.

Thirty-one essays, including Dennis H. Wrong's contribution, "How Important Is Social Class?", which contends that any serious effort at radical reconstruction of American society must start with the premise that workers and their institutions form a crucial force for social change."

Jencks, Christopher; Smith, Marshal; Acland, Henry; Bane, Mary Jo; Cohen, David; Gintis, Herbert; Heyns, Barbara; and Michelson, Stephan. *Inequality: A Reassessment of the Effect of Family and Schooling in America*. New York: Basic Books, 1972.

A pioneering and controversial study of the limits of education, as traditionally provided in the United States, as a tool for social mobility. Among the first volumes written by a liberal that acknowledges the importance of heredity on educational performance, the book has angered many. The message regarding inequality is clear, however: If you want equality, it is necessary to redistribute income.

Kuhns, William. *The Post-Industrial Prophets, Interpretations of Technology*. New York: Weybright and Talley, 1971.

Wrestles with the questions: What is technology? What are the routes of technological change? What, if any, are the boundaries of such change, and how do we evaluate it?

Lerner, Michael P. *The New Socialist Revolution. An Introduction to Its Theory and Strategy*. New York: Dell, 1973.

A sympathetic and engaging effort to explain why a socialist revolution is necessary in the United States, who will make that revolution, what its strategy should be, and what American society will be like under socialism. Among others, Lerner considers the questions of whether or not American society can be re-formed through the electoral process, and whether the Left will disappear after the Vietnam War is settled.

Lundberg, Ferdinand. *The Rich and the Super-Rich: A Study in the Power of Money Today*. New York: Bantam, 1969.

"A blistering attack on America's silent multimillionaire rulers who pay no taxes and run the country as tightly as any dictatorship."

Miller, Herman P. *Rich Man, Poor Man*. New York: Thomas Y. Crowell, 1971.

A clear and well-documented study of the distribution of income in America, by one of the nation's leading experts on census information.

Miller, S. M. and Roby, Pamela. *The Future of Inequality.* New York: Basic Books, 1970.

A lucid and pioneering analysis of the dimensions of inequality in America. The authors represent a productive new interdisciplinary trend among social scientists toward the sophisticated study of "social policy."

Moynihan, Daniel P. *The Politics of Guaranteed Income.*

An insider's view of the failure of welfare reform in the Nixon years. Moynihan blames both liberals and conservatives for this process, and sees the experience in the context of a general failure of the American political system to generate enlightened but incremental social reform.

Nader, Ralph and Ross, Donald. *Action for a Change: A Student's Manual for Public Interest Organizing.* New York: Grossman, 1971.

Addressed to the questions of "What can I do to improve my community?" and "How do I go about doing it?" Explores the mechanics of taking a serious abuse, laying it bare before the public, proposing solutions, and generating the necessary coalitions to see these solutions through. Especially urges students to form public interest research groups to help promote "initiatory democracy."

Parkin, Frank. *Class Inequality and Political Order.* New York: Praeger, 1971.

A comparative study of inequality in capitalist and communist societies, which emphasizes the varying roles of mass working-class parties.

Shostak, Arthur B. *Blue-Collar Life.* New York: Random House, 1969.

Wrestles with four related questions: Is the working class as well off as others believe? Is the life-style of stable blue-collarites an unequivocal answer to the plight of the nation's poor? Is the American manual worker truly disappearing as a separate and distinct social, psychological, and political entity? And is there anything that social planning and deliberate social change can contribute to the blue-collar pursuit of the "good life"?

Weisberg, Barry. *Beyond Repair: The Ecology of Capitalism.* Boston: Beacon Press, 1971.

"The Chamber of Commerce's worst fears about the ecology movement have materialized in [this new book]. . . . [It] offers a radical critique of corporate America . . . has created a mental exercise for the conservation movement." (*The Washington Post,* from the book jacket.)

INDEX

Accumulated-wealth model of inequality, 17–18
Adams, Samuel, 40
Agriculture, Department of, 94
Aid to the Blind, 106, 107, 121
Aid to Families with Dependent Children (AFDC), 90, 106–8, 110–11, 119, 121
Aid to the Permanently and Totally Disabled, 106, 121
Antipoverty programs, 13, 54, 90-91, 98, 100, 128–29
Aptitude tests, 15, 16, 20, 135
Armstrong, Richard, 120
Askew, Reuben, 41

Baroni, Father Geno, 40
Birchism, 40
Black Power Movement, 75
Blacks, 15, 100
Blocked-opportunity theory, 130, 133–34
Bond, Julian, 45
Bowles, Samuel, 19, 135
Burns, Eveline, 114
Bushmen, 1, 2

California Rural Legal Assistance, 96
Capitalism, 26–28, 52, 65, 66, 71, 100, 130, 137–40
Casework services, 13
Cash grants, 58, 92, 107–8
Cash-transfer programs, 98, 104, 108–24
Children's allowances, 114, 115
Citizen participation, 95
Class action suits, 96
Class subculture, concept of, 23–25
Classical economic theory, 99–100
Cleaver, Eldridge, 83
Cobb, Jonathan, 64
Cognitive model of inequality, 17
Cognitive skill, 15, 16, 18, 20
Columbo, Joe, 79
Committee on Economic Security, 105
Common Cause Movement, 40
Communism, 71
Community Action Programs (CAP), 91, 95–96
Community control, 95
Comparative perspective, inequality in, 26–28
Conflict perspective on inequality, 5–7
Congress, U.S., 101, 108
    welfare legislation, 90–91, 110, 111, 121
Congress of Industrial Organizations, 40
Consensus perspective on inequality, 4–6
Consensus theory of stratification, 134
Conservatism, 33–37, 74, 88, 119
Constitutionalism, 7
Consumers, 33, 35, 36
Conyers, John, 45
Corporations, 12, 42, 56–57
Credit income tax, 123–24, 140

Culture-of-poverty theory, 14, 23, 90, 127–30, 133–34
Cybernation, 69

Davis, Kingsley, 134
Day-care centers, 13
Dellums, Ron, 45
Democracy, participatory, 60–62
Democratic Party, 41, 47, 86, 111
Democratic socialist movement, 51–73, 74
    reform agenda, 53–62, 69
    utopianism, 65–68
    working class and, 62–65
Demogrants, 114, 116, 122–24
Discrimination, 13

Economic dualism, 26
Economic incentives, see Work incentives
Economic Opportunity Act of 1964, 91, 95
Education, 12–13, 16–17, 19–20, 89, 100, 129
Egalitarian societies, 1, 2
Elites, 5, 7, 21–22, 41, 137
Employment, 54–55, 96–101, 130–31
Employment Act of 1946, 97
Engels, Friedrich, 70
Enloe, Cynthia H., 74
Ethnicity, 75–86

Family Assistance Plan (FAP), 94, 99, 101, 110–11, 119–21, 129
Family socialization, 15
Federal Housing Administration, 93
Food programs, 94
Friedman, Milton, 109, 110, 114, 118

Gans, Herbert J., 23, 131–32, 139, 141
Gardner, John, 40
Gemeinschaft, 65
Geneen, Harold, 45
General Accounting Office, 99
Gintis, Herbert, 19, 135
Goldwater, Barry, 117
Goldwaterism, 40
Great Britain, 27, 28
Great Depression, 97, 104
Great Society, 69
Green, Mrs., 95
Green Amendment, 95
Greenfield, Jeff, 39, 41, 43
Groppi, Father James, 40

Hacker, Andrew, 68
Hannerz, Ulf, 23
Harrington, Michael, 51, 52, 55, 56, 58–60, 62–68, 70, 71
Harris, Fred, 39, 40, 41, 110, 114
Hart, Philip, 40
Head Start, 91
Health, Education and Welfare, Department of, 63–64
Health care, 13–14, 92–93
Heilbroner, Robert L., 137
Hicks, Louise Day, 86

148

Index

Hillquit, Morris, 71
Housing Act of 1968, 93
Housing programs, 13, 93–94
Howell, Henry, 41
Humphrey, Hubert, 116
Hunter-gatherer society, 1–3, 6, 7

Incentives, *see* Work incentives
Income:
    distribution of, 9–13, 17, 27–31
    guaranteed annual, 45, 58
    redistribution, 42–43, 58–59, 104–24, 138
Industrial urban society, 6, 7
Inflation, 97, 130–31
Inheritance, 16, 27, 34, 58
Internal Revenue Service (IRS), 57–58, 108, 109, 117
I.Q. test, 15, 20, 135

Jackson, Andrew, 40
Japan, 28
Jefferson, Thomas, 40
Jencks, Christopher, 15, 16–17, 28, 134
Job Corps, 91
Job creation, 96–97
Job training, 90, 98–99, 129
JOBS program, 99
Johnson, Lyndon B., 69

Kahane, Rabbi, 83
Kennedy, Edward, 40
Kennedy, John F., 79
Kennedy, Robert, 40, 79
King, Martin Luther, Jr., 40, 79
Kolko, Gabriel, 19
Kuznets, Simon, 9

La Follette, Robert, 40
Labor, Department of, 96
Labor, division of, 3, 4
Lampman, Robert J., 110, 114
Lasch, Christopher, 41, 46
Law enforcement, 43
Legal services, 13, 14, 96
Leisure, 69
Lekachman, Robert, 58–59
Lenski, Gerhard, 6–7
Liberalism, 33–37, 47, 53, 69, 74, 88, 119–20
Liebow, Elliot, 23
Long, Russell B., 119, 134
Lowrey, Bette, 85
Lucas, Robert E., 28

Macdonald, Dwight, 86
McGovern, George, 41, 48
McGovern Proposal, 114, 116, 123–24
Manpower Development and Training Act of 1962, 91, 98
Marcuse, Herbert, 66–68
Marx, Karl, 3, 5, 22–23, 63, 65, 66, 70, 130
Media, 82
Medicaid, 93, 96
Medicare, 93
Mikulski, Barbara, 86
Miller, S. M., 17
Mills, C. Wright, 41
Mills, Wilbur, 119
Minimum wage legislation, 97–98
Mobility, *see* Social mobility

Mohammed, Elijah, 83
Money, abolition of, 69–70
Moore, Wilbert E., 134
Mortgage-insurance programs, 93
Motivation, 4
Moynihan, Daniel P., 110, 132
Muckrackers, 40
Myrdal, Gunnar, 15–16

Nader, Ralph, 40
National Alliances of Businessmen, 99
Nationalization, 56–57
Negative income tax, 58, 108–10, 114, 117–18, 122, 123
Negative Wage Tax, 98
Neighborhood Youth Corps, 91, 98
Netherlands, 27
New Careers program, 98
New Left, 41
New Populism, 39–49, 66, 74, 75
Newfeld, Jack, 39, 41, 43
Nixon, Richard M., 36, 91, 94, 96, 101, 110, 120, 121
Novak, Michael, 74, 77, 79, 83
Nugent, Walter T., 41

Occupational status, 15, 19, 22
Office of Economic Opportunity (OEO), 93, 95, 96, 98
Old-Age, Survivors, Disability, and Health Insurance (OASDHI), 92, 110
Old-Age, Survivors, and Disability Insurance (OASDI), 110, 114, 115, 116
Old-Age Assistance, 106, 107, 119, 121
On-the-job training (OJT), 98–99
Oppenheimer, Martin, 60

Paine, Tom, 40
Participatory democracy, 60–62
Police, 43
Pollack, Norman, 41
Poor laws, 115, 118
Populism, 36–37, 40, 44, 85–86
    See also New Populism
Populist Manifesto: The Making of a New Majority, A (Newfeld and Greenfield), 39, 41
"Positive Functions of Poverty, The" (Gans), 131–32
Poverty:
    blocked-opportunity model, 130, 133–34
    culture of, 14, 23, 90, 127–30, 133–34
    income strategy, 92–94
    job strategy, 96–101
    power strategy, 94–96
    self-respect, 14–15
    service strategy, 13–14, 18, 90–91, 108
    stratification system, 134–36
Preindustrial urban society, 6, 7, 26
President's Commission on Income Maintenance Programs, 129
Proud'hon, Pierre Joseph, 5
Proxmire, William, 40
Public assistance, *see* Welfare
Public-housing programs, 13, 89
Pygmies, 1, 2

Race separatism, 45, 48
Racism, 46

Rainwater, Lee, 140
Ranking, 2, 3, 15
Reagan, Ronald, 96
Ribicoff, Abraham, 110, 114
Roby, Pamela, 17
Rockefeller, John D., 58
Rogin, Michael P., 41
Roles, specialization of, 3, 4
Rolph, Earl R., 123
Roosevelt, Franklin D., 40
Rousseau, Jean-Jacques, 3

Scarcity, 70
School-lunch program, 94
Schorr, Alvin, 107
Schultz, George, 99
Seeley, John, 23
Self-respect, 14–15, 18
Sennett, Richard, 64
Service model of inequality, 18
Service strategy, 13–14, 18, 90–91, 108
Smith, Adam, 35
Social class, 16, 22–26, 46
    See also Working class
Social insurance, see Social security
Social mobility, 21–22, 28
Social planning, 55, 57
Social security, 89, 105–7, 117
Social Security Act, 90–93, 105–7, 115, 121
Social Security Administration, 121
Socialism, 36–37, 52, 53, 65, 66, 70, 71, 75
    See also Democratic socialist movement
Socialism (Harrington), 65
Stratification system, 2, 3, 132, 134–36
Surplus-food program, 94
Sweden, 27, 28, 138

Talmadge Amendments, 91
Taxation, 34, 42, 45, 58–60, 108–10, 114, 117–18, 122–24, 138–40
Thomas, Norman, 51

Thurow, Lester C., 12, 28
Tierra del Fuego Indians, 1
Tobin, James, 58, 110, 114
Toffler, Alvin, 83
Transfer model of inequality, 17
Truman, Harry S, 40

Unemployment, 97, 98, 130–31, 138
Unemployment Insurance, 92, 105, 115, 116
United Mine Workers Union, 40
Utopianism, 65–68

Veterans Administration, 93

Wage differentials, theories of, 99–101
Wallace, George, 41, 85–86
War on Poverty, 91, 98–99
Ward, Lester Frank, 40
Warner, W. Lloyd, 23
Wealth, distribution of, 11, 12, 16, 17, 19
Weber, Max, 22–23
Welfare programs, 2, 89, 104–24, 131, 136
Welfare reform, 119–21
Welfare state, 27, 28, 52–53, 71, 88–89
West Germany, 28
White ethnics, 45, 76–86
Wilcox, Clair, 33–36
Wilson, James Q., 45
Wootton, Barbara, 100
Work, abolition of compulsory, 69–70
Work in America (HEW)), 63–64
Work Experience and Training Program, 91, 98
Work Incentive Program (WIN), 91
Work incentives, 35, 91, 109, 111, 117–19, 140, 141
Working class, 23, 24, 61–65, 76–86, 100
Works Progress Administration (WPA), 97

Yablonski family, 79
Young, Michael, 134–35